W9-DJH-983

Civil Liberties

Other books in the Current Controversies series:

Civil Liberties

James D. Torr, *Book Editor*

Daniel Leone, *President*
Bonnie Szumski, *Publisher*
Scott Barbour, *Managing Editor*
Helen Cothran, *Senior Editor*

CURRENT CONTROVERSIES

GREENHAVEN
PRESS ®

THOMSON
™
GALE

San Diego • Detroit • New York • San Francisco • Cleveland
New Haven, Conn. • Waterville, Maine • London • Munich

For more information, contact
Greenhaven Press
27500 Drake Rd.
Farmington Hills, MI 48331-3535
Or you can visit our Internet site at http://www.gale.com

LIBRARY OF CONGRESS CATALOGING-IN-PUBLICATION DATA

Civil liberties / James D. Torr, book editor.
    p. cm. — (Current controversies)
Includes bibliographical references and index.
ISBN 0-7377-1465-4 (pbk. : alk. paper) — ISBN 0-7377-1464-6 (lib. : alk. paper)
    1. Civil rights—United States. 2. National security—United States. 3.
Terrorism—United States—Prevention. I. Torr, James D., 1974– . II. Series.
JC599.U5 C546 2003
323'.0973—dc21
                                              2002027151

Contents

Chapter 1: Should Limits Be Placed on Freedom of Expression?

Yes: Censorship Is Justified in Certain Circumstances

No: Censorship Violates the First Amendment

Chapter 2: Does Separation of Church and State Threaten Religious Liberty?

Yes: Strict Enforcement of the Separation of Church and State Threatens Religious Liberty

Chapter 4: Does the Threat of Terrorism Justify Curtailment of Civil Liberties?

Yes: Americans Should Sacrifice Some Freedoms in Times of Crisis

No: National Security Should Not Come at the Expense of Civil Liberties

Foreword

By definition, controversies are "discussions of questions in which opposing opinions clash" (Webster's Twentieth Century Dictionary Unabridged). Few would deny that controversies are a pervasive part of the human condition and exist on virtually every level of human enterprise. Controversies transpire between individuals and among groups, within nations and between nations. Controversies supply the grist necessary for progress by providing challenges and challengers to the status quo. They also create atmospheres where strife and warfare can flourish. A world without controversies would be a peaceful world; but it also would be, by and large, static and prosaic.

The Series' Purpose

The purpose of the Current Controversies series is to explore many of the social, political, and economic controversies dominating the national and international scenes today. Titles selected for inclusion in the series are highly focused and specific. For example, from the larger category of criminal justice, Current Controversies deals with specific topics such as police brutality, gun control, white collar crime, and others. The debates in Current Controversies also are presented in a useful, timeless fashion. Articles and book excerpts included in each title are selected if they contribute valuable, long-range ideas to the overall debate. And wherever possible, current information is enhanced with historical documents and other relevant materials. Thus, while individual titles are current in focus, every effort is made to ensure that they will not become quickly outdated. Books in the Current Controversies series will remain important resources for librarians, teachers, and students for many years.

In addition to keeping the titles focused and specific, great care is taken in the editorial format of each book in the series. Book introductions and chapter prefaces are offered to provide background material for readers. Chapters are organized around several key questions that are answered with diverse opinions representing all points on the political spectrum. Materials in each chapter include opinions in which authors clearly disagree as well as alternative opinions in which authors may agree on a broader issue but disagree on the possible solutions. In this way, the content of each volume in Current Controversies mirrors the mosaic of opinions encountered in society. Readers will quickly realize that there are many viable answers to these complex issues. By questioning each author's conclusions, students and casual readers can begin to develop the critical thinking skills so important to evaluating opinionated material.

Current Controversies is also ideal for controlled research. Each anthology in the series is composed of primary sources taken from a wide gamut of informational categories including periodicals, newspapers, books, United States and foreign government documents, and the publications of private and public organizations. Readers will find factual support for reports, debates, and research papers covering all areas of important issues. In addition, an annotated table of contents, an index, a book and periodical bibliography, and a list of organizations to contact are included in each book to expedite further research.

Perhaps more than ever before in history, people are confronted with diverse and contradictory information. During the Persian Gulf War, for example, the public was not only treated to minute-to-minute coverage of the war, it was also inundated with critiques of the coverage and countless analyses of the factors motivating U.S. involvement. Being able to sort through the plethora of opinions accompanying today's major issues, and to draw one's own conclusions, can be a complicated and frustrating struggle. It is the editors' hope that Current Controversies will help readers with this struggle.

Greenhaven Press anthologies primarily consist of previously published material taken from a variety of sources, including periodicals, books, scholarly journals, newspapers, government documents, and position papers from private and public organizations. These original sources are often edited for length and to ensure their accessibility for a young adult audience. The anthology editors also change the original titles of these works in order to clearly present the main thesis of each viewpoint and to explicitly indicate the opinion presented in the viewpoint. These alterations are made in consideration of both the reading and comprehension levels of a young adult audience. Every effort is made to ensure that Greenhaven Press accurately reflects the original intent of the authors included in this anthology.

Introduction

One of the major questions in the aftermath of the September 11, 2001, terrorist attacks on America is what effects the U.S. war on terror will have on Americans' civil liberties. Within days of the attacks, some pundits and public officials began calling for expanded police, FBI, and CIA powers to combat future attacks. They were quickly answered by commentators who warned that to turn the United States into a police state would be to give the enemies of democracy a partial victory. "If we are intimidated to the point of restricting our freedoms, the terrorists will have won," said American Civil Liberties Union (ACLU) executive director Anthony D. Romero in January 2002.

History shows that curtailment of civil liberties—including the right to free speech, the right to a fair trial, and the right to equal protection under the law—has often followed national crises. During the Civil War, Abraham Lincoln suspended the writ of habeus corpus on several occasions, holding suspected traitors without trial even though only Congress can authorize such action. During World War I, more than 1,100 people were jailed or fined under the Sedition Act, which essentially made it a crime to criticize the government or the war effort. The law was later declared unconstitutional. In 1918, a series of strikes, riots, and bombings culminated in the Palmer raids: Gross civil liberties violations ensued as law enforcement officials led raids on suspected radicals in dozens of cities, arresting more than 6,000 people, many without a warrant.

After September 11, a consensus emerged that, as much as possible, the war on terrorism should be waged without the civil liberties violations that have occurred in prior crises. For example, one of the nations' worst overreactions to a national emergency occurred after the bombing of Pearl Harbor, when the U.S. government evacuated more than 120,000 Japanese Americans from the West Coast and held them in internment camps. In the wake of September 11, U.S. leaders took active steps to avoid a similar episode. "How different [from the atmosphere after the attack on Pearl Harbor]," writes Harvard law professor Laurence H. Tribe, "was the sight of New York's Mayor Rudolph Giuliani, soon followed by President Bush, appealing eloquently to Americans not to seek revenge on their fellow citizens who happened to be Muslims."

Nevertheless, Americans' civil liberties will surely be affected by the aftermath of September 11. Some substantial changes have already been made. A bill called the Uniting and Strengthening America by Providing Appropriate

Tools Required to Intercept and Obstruct Terrorism Act of 2001—also known as the Patriot Act—was passed by Congress late in 2001 to help the antiterrorism effort. Among other things, the law:

- allows the government to detain any foreigners whom the attorney general has "reasonable grounds to believe" might be a threat to national security.
- eases officials' ability to eavesdrop on communications between lawyers and their clients in federal custody when it would "deter future acts of violence or terrorism."
- expands federal agents' power to conduct telephone and e-mail surveillance.
- enhances the ability of federal agents to conduct "sneak-and-peek" searches, in which agents search an individual's home without notifying them.

President George Bush has also, through an executive order, authorized the use of military tribunals—in which defendants are stripped of many traditional legal protections—to try suspected terrorists.

While most of these curtailments on civil liberties are directed at suspected terrorists, average Americans may be affected in other, less direct ways. For example, a wartime atmosphere has historically had a chilling effect on free expression. In a widely publicized case, the University of New Mexico disciplined a history professor for jokingly telling a class on September 11 that "anyone who can blow up the Pentagon gets my vote." And more than a dozen ABC affiliates pulled comedian Bill Maher's *Politically Incorrect* talk show after Maher remarked on September 17 that "we have been the cowards lobbing cruise missiles from 2,000 miles away," referring to U.S. bombings of Iraq since the Persian Gulf War. "That's cowardly. Staying in the airplane while it hits the building, say what you want about it, it's not cowardly." Civil libertarians worry that incidents like these will create an atmosphere in which people are afraid to criticize the government.

The right to privacy may also be compromised, as law enforcement agencies intensify their efforts to identify and track suspicious individuals. Airline travelers have submitted to more frequent random searches, although proposals to issue national ID cards have met with substantial public opposition. Facial recognition technology systems—which use surveillance cameras and a computer database of photographs to identify individuals in a crowd—have already been installed in several airports, and there have been proposals to implement retinal-scan technology as well. Critics of this increased surveillance have compared it to George Orwell's classic novel *1984*, which depicts a totalitarian society in which "Big Brother"—the government—is always watching. Security experts, on the other hand, insist that such measures are necessary and that they will not be abused.

In the end, the intense debate over the effects of antiterrorism efforts on civil liberties may itself be the best sign that Americans' constitutional rights will survive the current crisis. History shows that civil liberties are often abused in times of national crisis, but it also shows that civil liberties have survived those crises. The viewpoints in *Current Controversies: Civil Liberties* debate the importance of civil liberties and the potential threats to them in the following chapters: Should Limits Be Placed on Freedom of Expression? Does Separation of Church and State Threaten Religious Liberty? Is the Right to Privacy Threatened? Does the Threat of Terrorism Justify Curtailment of Civil Liberties? The wide range of opinions in these chapters demonstrates that while Americans as a whole cherish the freedoms guaranteed in the Constitution, they hold strong and differing views on how those freedoms should be exercised and whether or not they should be restricted.

Chapter 1

Should Limits Be Placed on Freedom of Expression?

Chapter Preface

The sale of pornographic materials has long been one of the most contentious issues surrounding the right to free speech—and the rapid spread of online pornography has intensified this debate. Critics argue that online pornography makes indecent material more pervasive and easily accessible than ever before. They emphasize how easy it is for children to access such material.

The courts have traditionally upheld adults' rights to view pornography, while also allowing laws that protect children from it. Free speech advocates, however, maintain that it is very difficult to use this type of regulatory framework on the Internet. Due to the nature of the medium, any attempt to limit children's access to objectionable material will unavoidably limit adults' access to it as well, undermining free expression on the web.

The federal government's first attempt to deal with Internet pornography was the 1996 Communications Decency Act (CDA), which made it a crime to send sexually explicit messages to anyone under eighteen. The Supreme Court struck down the law in 1997, however, on the grounds that it was too broad and vague in its definition of what types of messages were prohibited.

In 1998 Congress tried to avoid the flaws of the CDA with the Child Online Protection Act (COPA). The law provides a narrower definition of what is banned: material depicting "sexual acts" and "lewd acts" that the "average person, applying contemporary community standards, would find . . . is designed . . . to pander to the prurient interest and . . . lacks serious literary, artistic, political, or scientific value to minors." The wording of the law harkens back to the 1973 Supreme Court decision *Miller v. California*, which distinguished between pornography, which the Court held is protected by the First Amendment, and obscenity, which is not. Pornography consists of erotic or sexually explicit material, while obscenity, according to the Supreme Court, is 1) sexually explicit, 2) offensive according to "contemporary community standards," and 3) lacking in literary, artistic, or political value.

Free speech advocates have objected to the "community standards" criterion as it pertains to the Internet. The American Civil Liberties Union, for example, argued that under COPA the community standards of the most conservative towns in America could be used to shut down websites that are not offensive to most of the country. Agreeing with this logic, a federal court in Philadelphia blocked COPA from taking effect. In May 2002, however, the Supreme Court overturned the lower court's decision, ruling that it is not unconstitutional to use "contemporary community standards" to define obscenity.

The debate over COPA is by no means over, as free speech advocates have filed several other challenges to the law. The viewpoints in the following chapter further explore the pornography controversy and other free speech issues.

Censorship of Violence in Popular Entertainment Is Justified

by Robert Peters

About the author: *Robert Peters is president of Morality in the Media, a national nonprofit organization established in 1962 to combat obscenity and uphold decency standards in the media.*

My name is Robert Peters. I am a graduate of Dartmouth and N.Y.U. School of Law. I began my work at Morality in Media in May 1985 as a staff attorney, and I was named president in September 1992. Founded in New York City in 1962, Morality in Media is a national, not-for-profit, interfaith organization that works through constitutional means to combat obscenity ("hard-core pornography") and to uphold standards of decency in the media.

We are also concerned about the related problem of gratuitous (and often graphic, sadistic) violence in various media: TV, films, music/RAP, video and computer games.

That violence occurs in real life, no one can deny; and few would argue that the media should never, under any circumstances, depict or describe an act of deadly or injurious violence.

I recently watched "Glory," a film about the heroic efforts of African American Union soldiers in the Civil War. I wouldn't recommend the film for small children, but the film's graphic violence was not gratuitous. Many PBS documentaries about the two World Wars of this century have depicted the horror of war. I wouldn't recommend them for small children, but none depicted violence in a gratuitous manner. "Private Ryan" and "Schindler's List" also depict horrific violence; but again, the purpose is to instruct, not sensationalize.

While I have often wondered why the "crime of choice" for drama is usually murder (often multiple murders), it is clear that drama can treat the details of murder in an essentially responsible manner. One technique is to not show the murderous conduct.

Excerpted from Robert Peters's testimony before the New Jersey State Legislature Assembly Task Force on Adolescent Violence, Trenton, New Jersey, January 20, 1999.

Chapter 1

Gratuitous, Easily Imitated Violence

As I see it, however, there are four big problems with media violence. The first problem is that there is too much of it. Dr. George Gerbner, dean-emeritus of the Annenberg School of Communication at the University of Pennsylvania, has been the most eloquent spokesperson for the view that, apart from any causal connection to real life violence, the glut of media violence desensitizes viewers and contributes to the "mean world syndrome."

I would add that the glut of media violence also robs young people of valuable opportunities to view programs in which others successfully deal with real life problems without violence and participate in an infinite variety of constructive (or at least not injurious) and often rewarding activities. While some violent programs provide positive role models, few youth will become:

- police officers
- private detectives
- prosecutors
- defense attorneys who always represent the good guys
- vampire-slayers
- defenders against alien beings

A second problem with media violence is that much of it can easily be imitated. To help make the point, I will digress for a few moments to my own childhood.

I was born in 1949 and raised in a small town in Illinois. Back then, there was plenty of violence in films, but it consisted mostly of war violence, cowboy (and Indian) violence, good guy-bad guy violence (where the good guys always won) and horror films, like the "Monster from the Black Lagoon." I still have a picture of my brother and I with our cowboy hats on and six guns dangling from their holsters. I still remember the thrill of playing war games with a plastic carbine and wanting to be a "G-man." But there weren't opportunities to do away with other cowboys or hostile Indians, Germans or Japanese or with gangsters or monsters.

I would add that I grew up in a community where hunting was common and where many people, including my father, had a gun in the home. Killing each other or our classmates, teachers or neighbors, however, never entered our young, impressionable minds.

> *"Why should we be surprised to discover that kids now fantasize about injuring or killing . . . when that is what they are constantly exposed to?"*

Today, things are different. Gone are the industry standards that prevented film producers and directors from glorifying the bad guys; and the bad guys are no longer cowboys, hostile armies or denizens of the underworld or a black lagoon. They are often troubled, youthful characters with real life coun-

19

terparts found in our nation's troubled homes and communities, and they engage in behavior kids can readily imitate.

A third problem with today's media violence is the manner in which it is depicted. It is one thing to show a shooting or stabbing; it is another to show it in sadistic slow motion with the bullet(s) or knife penetrating the body, the blood spurting and a body part dangling or flying—and to do so, not for the purpose of showing the horror of violence, but rather to portray it as an exciting, pleasurable and effective way to handle problems.

I still remember as a child listening to football games on the radio, and anxiously waiting to go out and play football when the game was over. Why should we be surprised to discover that kids now fantasize about injuring or killing a peer, neighbor, retailer or cop—when that is what they are constantly exposed to and what is made so exciting and appealing?

The fourth problem with media violence is Hollywood's infatuation with guns. Instead of portraying guns as, at best, a necessary evil (when used as weapons), guns—especially handguns—are portrayed as a means of empowerment; as a component of being "tough" and/or a way to be in control of a situation. Why should we be surprised to discover that so many kids want a gun? If Hollywood stopped glorifying possession and use of handguns, there would be far fewer crimes committed by youth with handguns.

> *"[There should be] a law making it a crime to knowingly distribute or exhibit to minors entertainment that contains specified types of violence."*

The defenders of media violence often say that there is no conclusive scientific proof that media violence "causes" or contributes to real life criminal violence. This may be true, but that doesn't mean there isn't a large body of evidence showing a connection between media violence and real life violence.

I often say that when common sense, personal experience, anecdotal evidence and social science research all point in the same direction, the burden of proof should shift from those who argue that there is a connection to those who say there isn't.

Clearly, common sense indicates there is a connection. Kids learn not only by observing or listening to persons who are actually in their physical presence but also from observing or listening to what they see or hear on film or TV or video or computer. Most of us also know from personal experiences that kids learn from and imitate what they watch or hear on film or TV or video or audio recordings; and it wasn't always good!

There is also a mountain of anecdotal evidence, often found in local newspaper accounts of crimes, which indicates that viewing antisocial behavior on film, TV or a video/computer game or listening to antisocial behavior being extolled in music or RAP lyrics negatively affect many young people. Finally, there is a mountain of social science research showing a link between viewing antisocial behavior on TV and real life anti-social behavior.

Reducing the Amount of Violence in Popular Entertainment

What then can society do about the problem of media violence? Part of the answer is unquestionably a greater effort to raise public awareness. In particular, parents, educators and clergy must be made to understand that youth are often negatively affected by what they see and hear in "popular culture," and that every reasonable effort must be made to shield youth from harmful media influences and to educate youth about how media affects them.

Every effort must also be made to impress upon those that produce and distribute entertainment that along with their rights comes a weighty responsibility to exercise those rights in a manner that does not carelessly or recklessly cause harm to others. If efforts at moral persuasion fail, the finger of public disapproval and, whenever possible, economic persuasion, must also be brought to bear. While public officials cannot do the whole job, their added voice will strengthen the grass roots efforts.

The last remedy is the law. Personally, I would much rather see the media voluntarily get its house in order, without resort to law. But if the media fails or refuses to accept its responsibility, then I would suggest two different legal approaches to address the problems.

The first is a law making it a crime to knowingly distribute or exhibit to minors entertainment that contains specified types of violence. While the courts have often invalidated such laws [see, e.g., *Interstate Circuit v. City of Dallas,* 396 U.S. 676 (1968); *Video Software Dealers Association v. Webster,* 968 F.2d 684 (8th Cir. 1992)], the Supreme Court has never held that the Constitution forbids all laws restricting children's access to media violence. The challenge, as I see it, is in the drafting.

The second approach would make those who distribute media violence civilly liable, in limited circumstances, for the foreseeable harms that result. The courts have not looked favorably on efforts to hold media companies civilly responsible for such injuries; and, to some extent, with good reason. No matter how responsibly a media company acts, there is always the possibility that some tormented soul or depraved sociopath might get the wrong idea. And even responsible people can at times make errors in judgment. Clearly, the barrier for establishing liability would have to be somewhat high. But in my view, it is unconscionable to let media companies off the hook, no matter how irresponsibly or recklessly or with depraved indifference they act, unless they legally "incite" the conduct. There simply must be a rule of reason in this area of law, which has so far eluded the courts.

I should add that in my view, a law requiring content ratings on destructive garbage may help a relatively few parents, but content ratings alone will not solve the problems.

In conclusion, I am not here to indict the media for all or even most of the violent, antisocial behavior that occurs in society. Clearly, other causes are at work—including drugs, the proliferation of handguns, dysfunctional families and the vicious cycle of poverty. But to go to the other extreme and to argue that "popular culture" is not a factor, is at best a display of ignorance and at worst a purposeful attempt to deceive the public and this Task Force.

As I see it, there is no one easy solution to the problem; but a concerted effort on the part of all concerned will bring meaningful progress and, in the long run, spare many youth, as well as their families, peers, neighbors and communities, much heartbreak and tragedy.

Censorship of Pornography May Be Justified

by Holman W. Jenkins Jr.

About the author: *Holman W. Jenkins Jr. is a member of the editorial board of the* Wall Street Journal.

Pornography is not a subject one would expect to come up at a baby shower. But there I was when two Manhattan women of my acquaintance began discussing the web surfing habits of their husbands. It seems they had discovered the "history" folder on their spouses' web browsers. That's the folder that (unless you turn it off) maintains a list of web sites visited over the previous month or so. When they clicked, it popped open and revealed a list of porn sites running off the bottom of the screen.

What struck them most was the sheer astonishing breadth and variety of the porn trove. Tastes and fetishes that they wouldn't have guessed existed are catered to by an endless universe of smut purveyors. They giggled over their discovery, disapproving but not terribly so. When one of the husbands came over, he giggled too. No harm done, right?

This came even as the [2000] presidential campaign was making a strange sidelong excursion into panic about sex and violence (mostly violence) in the mainstream media. The Federal Trade Commission [FTC] had just issued a report blaming Hollywood for marketing R-rated fare to children as young as eight.

The cacophony was deafening. Hearings were held before John McCain's Senate Commerce Committee. Hollywood executives were pilloried, denounced, and held up to public ignominy. Al Gore and Joe Lieberman promised that, if elected, they would give the entertainment industry six months to shape up—or else.

Of course, what "or else" meant was never clear. In quieter moments legislators admitted "or else" was nothing, because Washington wasn't about to get into the censorship business. Within a month of the election, the same FTC that had started the blaze solemnly pronounced that it had no intention of doing anything about the "abuses" it had uncovered. Nor would it advise Congress to do anything. This utter failure to propose a remedy was all the more striking when considered against the rhetoric the politicians had been spilling out a few weeks earlier, implying that entertainment violence was responsible for everything from the massacre at Columbine High School in Colorado to scholastic underachievement. Lieberman never missed a chance on the campaign trail to repeat his top applause line: "Parents shouldn't be forced to compete with popular culture to raise their children."

Misplaced Concern over Media Violence

Alarm over "sex and violence" in popular entertainment has been a recurring theme for at least a century. Yet it seems to recur without any progress in our understanding of the subject.

In fact, there is no reliable evidence of any causal link between imaginary violence in entertainment and violence in the real world. The nation has been witnessing a stark drop in the rates of murder, rape, and violent crime since the early 1990s. Does anyone suppose this was caused by a decline in violent themes in movies, TV shows, and video games?

Likewise, there has been a less striking but still significant decline in teenage motherhood, the spread of sexual diseases, and other indicators of promiscuity. We certainly can't credit this to any decline in the number of plot lines on "Friends" and other NBC sitcoms extolling the desirability of frequent casual sexual relationships. There is no question that a long-term transformation of sexual mores has been underway for decades, thanks to the pill, sex education, and so forth. Yes, the media undoubtedly serve as a transmission belt for changing attitudes. But that's a far cry from suggesting that people act on what they see in the media in a monkey-see, monkey-do manner.

Indeed, when you think about it, the assumption that sex in the entertainment media leads to sex in the world, or that violence leads to violence, is methodologically fishy. What foundation does this have except for a casual, intuitive belief that the imaginary must lead to the real? It seems just as plausible that imaginary sex might lead to violence or imaginary violence to sex. Or both might lead to shopping. The logic is not only questionable, but in a society as surfeited with every kind of entertainment as ours, the evidence that would allow any strong conclusion about the relationship between entertainment and social pathology is noticeably absent.

"Internet porn . . . has emerged as a major threat to marriages."

In fact, we know from the work of James Hamilton, an economist at Duke University, that the demand for violence in entertainment comes most strongly from young adults of both sexes. His study of Nielsen data shows that those most likely to tune into TV movies with violent themes are, first, males aged 18 to 34, then females aged 18 to 34. Both older and younger viewers are less interested in mayhem. Beyond doubt the big entertainment companies have figured this out, too. Young adults are their most prized demographic, the ones brand-name advertisers pay the most to reach. Yet if there seems to be a proliferation of violent entertainment, it's mostly illusory. Violent shows are less a staple of prime-time network fare than they were two decades ago (having been replaced, interestingly, by lawyer shows). Instead there has been a proliferation of all kinds of entertainment, as the multiplication

> *"Respectable companies like AT&T, Time-Warner, and the Hilton hotel chain have quietly become major players in porn distribution."*

of cable channels allows programming to be targeted more narrowly at different audiences. Now violent fare can be served up with less fear of annoying the audience who find violence distasteful or offensive.

More speculative is the question of why young adults demand violent-theme entertainment. Dolf Zillman, a psychologist at the University of Alabama, has studied the question and proposed an answer: Violent entertainment is really about justice. A question that particularly concerns young people is whether good or evil triumphs in the world, whether virtue is rewarded and meanness is punished. And it doesn't take a great deal of art (always in short supply in Hollywood) to encapsulate these themes in plots that make extensive use of violence. This makes sense, if only because the sheer prevalence of violent themes in popular entertainment suggests it needs some kind of explanation tying it to universal human concerns.

The Porn Revolution

That's not to say there isn't plenty of room to criticize the entertainment media, but the focus ignores the proverbial elephant in the living room. While Republicans and Democrats were competing to see who could issue the most comprehensive denunciation of Hollywood depravity, they ignored an authentic and unprecedented phenomenon: the revolution in the availability of pornography.

Porn has moved out of a few segregated public spaces, the seedy book shops and triple-X theaters, and become ubiquitous on the web, on cable, in neighborhood video shops. Some consider this a good thing, since it promises to put the red-light districts of our downtown areas out of business. . . . But I'm not sure we're going to be happy with the bargain in the long run. The more accessible the material, the larger the number of people who will be willing to consume it (because they can do so discreetly). And here's where the consequences get worrisome: the larger and more scalable the market, the more it can supply material to dovetail with every individual quirk or taste. Given the way porn seems to act on those who are most susceptible to it, we may be surprised at the results.

Trying to point this out (believe me, I know) is to invite scorn from liberal entertainment crusaders who accuse conservatives of being more afraid of sex than violence. I wrote a column in the *Wall Street Journal* on the subject during the presidential campaign, and the letters that came in response more often than not criticized me for muddying an important national debate over the "serious" problem of violence in the media by raising irrelevant objections about pornography.

Yet these critics have it backwards, I fear. Nobody has heard of self-help groups for people claiming to be "addicted" to sexual innuendo on "Friends" or to violence in Arnold Schwarzenegger films. Yet in the past few years, not only have organizations popped into being to aid people who feel a compulsive "addiction" to view pornography; the subject has also begun to arise with alarming frequency in divorce and custody proceedings. Internet porn, at least in the collective mind of the counseling industry, has emerged as a major threat to marriages. What's more, if you have access to a newspaper database, you can find story after story about some locally prominent person being disgraced, arrested, or fired because of the discovery of a cache of porn on his home or office computer.

Such was the fate that recently befell a Harvard Divinity dean, a Disney Internet executive, countless college professors and school teachers, and other once-reputable citizens around the country. This is to say nothing of the mass firings that have rippled through numerous corporations (including the *New York Times*) after employees were caught misusing company computers to receive and distribute porn.

Dr. Mark Laaser, a co-founder of the Christian Alliance for Sexual Recovery (and himself a recovering "sex addict"), had this to say at a [2000] congressional hearing:

> Many in the medical community feel that for a substance or activity to be addictive it must create a chemical tolerance. Alcoholics know, for example, that over the lifetime of their addiction, they must consume more and more alcohol to achieve the same effect. New research, such as by Drs. Harvey Milkman and Stan Sunderwirth, has demonstrated that sexual fantasy and activity, because of naturally produced brain chemicals, has the ability to create brain tolerance to sex. I have treated over a thousand male and female sex addicts. Almost all of them began with pornography.

Whether the medicalization of the phenomenon is appropriate is a fair question. But if a significant number of people believe their lives are being disrupted by an addiction to pornography, that already puts porn in a different category from run-of-the-mill entertainment sex and violence. All by itself, the fact that some people are seeking help entitles us to conclude something new and different is going on.

Not Prosecuting Obscenity

That politicians would prefer to ignore the porn revolution and shout about a nonexistent crisis in media violence might seem a mystery at first. But media violence is a problem they're not really obliged to do anything about—that pesky amendment stands in the way. Plus, Hollywood is a powerful trade group. And the public clearly votes with its pocketbook in favor of the product.

To be sure, unstoppable technology plays a role in the ubiquity of pornography. But another factor is the near-collapse of obscenity enforcement since the Reagan-Bush years. Remember the Meese Commission on Pornography? Well, times surely changed with the arrival of the Clinton administration.

In the *New York Observer,* Dennis Hof, an associate of *Hustler* publisher Larry Flynt, gave as good a rendition of recent history as anyone could wish: "Here's what's happened. We've had eight years of lack of prosecution of a sex industry. Who's Bill Clinton going to prosecute with all his stuff going on? Janet Reno doesn't want any part of that. So the film industry has gone from 1,000 films eight years ago to 10,000 last year. Ten thousand pornographic movies. You've got Larry and [*Penthouse* publisher Bob] Guccione doing things that 10 years ago you'd go to prison for. Then you've got all the Internet stuff—dogs, horses, 12-year-old girls, all this crazed Third-World s— going on."

> *"[The spread of pornography] comes with a likely train of genuine social pathology whose limits we'll just have to discover."*

One reason the porn prosecutions dried up is that, shortly after taking office, Bill Clinton fired all the sitting U.S. attorneys. That wiped out an experienced cadre of prosecutors who had made obscenity a priority. Since then, the administration has focused exclusively on kiddie porn prosecutions, for all the obvious it-takes-a-village reasons. The Justice Department insists it's merely making more efficient use of its resources: And indeed, while previous administrations had their successes, many garden-variety obscenity cases certainly did end badly for the government. Judges and juries have not always been friendly. But the threat of prosecution at least had the salutary effect of discouraging mainstream companies from involving themselves in the porn racket. That has changed in a big way.

Wall Street once wouldn't have touched the business with a 10-foot pole. Now it may not brag about the association, but reputable brokerages have been glad to help porn-related companies win public listings on U.S. stock exchanges. Venture firms have been major backers of companies that provide billing and tracking services for on-line smut merchants. For that matter, Visa and Mastercard play a large role in the industry by processing its payments. (American Express recently stopped processing charges for "adult" sites, but the reason was the inordinate volume of "chargebacks" by customers who denied patronizing the sites when the bills came due.)

Though they don't advertise the connection, respectable companies like AT&T, Time-Warner, and the Hilton hotel chain have quietly become major players in porn distribution. A few years ago the cable TV folks wouldn't go near the stuff unless (as in New York City) the porn entrepreneurs managed to get on a mandated "public access" channel. The cable industry's resistance has now completely crumbled. Consider the success of Hot Network, provided by Steve Hirsch's Vivid Entertainment Group, the industry-leading producer of high-quality sex videos. Since its launch in 1999, Hot Network has taken the cable world by storm. As one cable executive anonymously told the *Journal's* Sally Beatty, "The No. 1 complaint we get is that it's not explicit enough."

America Online, in a sense, is one of the biggest beneficiaries of the Internet porn wave, even though it doesn't consider itself "in" the porn business. Yet in private moments, people at the company will acknowledge that a very large part of their subscriber traffic is people who use AOL to gain access to the pornucopia available on the Internet beyond AOL's own content sites.

So huge has the industry become that it now has its own glitzy award ceremony sponsored by its own glossy trade magazine, *Adult Video News*. The Defiance Haven resort, on the island of St. Maarten in the Caribbean, has launched a new business hosting a procession of "adult travel" package tours. For a hefty sum, fans can spend three days partying and socializing with their favorite porn queens. Last October, the lineup included sex stars Taylor Wane, Julia Parton, and Bianca Trump.

Whole genres of pop music are now in the process of coalescing with the "respectable" porn industry, most notably represented by Vivid, whose stable of Vivid Girls is much in demand for autograph signings at Tower Records and local video outlets. The

> *"Having unlimited porn imagery within easy reach of every computer is likely to produce social effects that we haven't yet reckoned with."*

New York Times recently noted the "creepy" fact that rap music, professional wrestling, and porn "have aligned to shape a real audience, one that looks awfully hardened." And both Fox News and MTV have invested airtime in exploring what Fox called the "rock-porn connection" (though MTV was comparatively weak on disapproval).

Nobody knows how big the industry is, though the most quoted estimate is about $5 billion in annual sales (with another $1 billion for Internet porn). *Adult Video News* claims sex videos, mostly produced in suburban Los Angeles neighborhoods like Chatsworth and Reseda, generate more in sales and rental revenues than legitimate Hollywood manages to earn at the domestic box office. Porn probably provides more employment for Hollywood's army of film technicians and set personnel than mainstream film production does.

America's Cultural Divide

Yet for all the fiery denunciations of mainstream Hollywood during the election campaign, even an acknowledgement of the porn industry's existence seemed almost taboo. This was strange. Wouldn't denouncing the porn explosion be a potential home run for any politician who might be seeking to ride America's renewed concern (as confirmed by every poll) with "values"?

One reason for the reluctance might be related to the cultural divide reflected in the election result (with Al Gore winning the heavily populated coasts, George Bush winning small-town and rural America). As Francis Fukuyama wrote in the *Wall Street Journal* shortly after the election, the division suggests that sexual mores after Bill Clinton have become a political minefield between two Americas that politicians have decided it's better to avoid:

> That conservatives held a losing hand in the culture wars became painfully evident during the Monica Lewinsky impeachment saga. There is hardly anyone in the country who approved of President Clinton's behavior. But a substantial number of Americans disliked the Republicans even more intensely for what they perceived to be moralism on this issue . . . [T]he perception remained that the Republicans were passing judgment on an area of personal behavior that was a matter of individual moral choice.

By acclamation, the one exception to the official blind eye is child pornography. Indeed, such is the enthusiasm to bust kiddie-porn miscreants that law enforcement has veered close to entrapment in some cases. The Disney executive's first trial ended in a hung jury for exactly this reason. As with the attack on mainstream media sex and violence, campaigners can present themselves as protecting children rather than policing the behavior of consenting adults.

Whatever the reason, the porn genie won't be stuffed back in the bottle. Yet this genie comes with a likely train of genuine social pathology whose limits we'll just have to discover. One can only speculate here, but pornographic sexual images are quite different from entertainment sex and violence: They are real. They are processed differently. The "suspension of disbelief" has always been baloney: The essential question for healthy psychological functioning is the ability to distinguish reality from fantasy. People watching a Schwarzenegger shoot-'em-up know it's make believe. That's why they can watch graphic depictions of murder and mayhem without flinching.

Likewise sexual quips on the typical TV sitcom, or even a steamy Sharon Stone scene, aren't arousing in the sense that pornography is. The fictional media don't play on the powerful chemical signals that real sexual stimuli activate, producing states of motivation so powerful they can temporarily overwhelm even strong sensations like hunger or fatigue. Now this stuff is coming into the homes of people who would otherwise never have encountered it. And porn lends itself to the power of digital technology, which can scale up a mass audience at virtually no additional cost per customer. Where it gets interesting, if that's the word, is that the same scalability allows more varied and narrow tastes to be served. If you have a susceptibility to, say, African American lesbians engaged in "water play" that you didn't know about, the web is the place to find out.

The people providing this material are a side of the business without the fixed addresses and scrubbed and healthy face of Vivid Entertainment and its Vivid Girls. In the early 1990s, the "mainstream" porn business got a black eye when one of its young stars, "Savannah," blew out her brains after a car accident. About the same time, another, Traci Lords, was revealed to have been underage when she made her films. Hundreds of thousands of dollars worth of her "product" had to be destroyed (and Lords, now reclothed as a "victim" of porn, went on to a career on network television, much to the annoyance of her former colleagues).

Since then, the "respectable" end of the porn business has made a point of hiring lobbyists, participating in charity, and campaigning for condoms against AIDS. There is no question that part of the industry has cleaned up its act. That, and its success at making celebrities out of a few leading porn stars, have made the industry increasingly acceptable company for the makers and marketers of mainstream pop culture.

But what about the other material, the "dogs, horses, 12-year-old girls, all this crazed Third-World s—"? To imagine that a great engine of exploitation and abuse doesn't lie behind this imagery is to live in a fantasy world. Just last year, for example, French porn star and 22-time surgical patient Lolo Ferrari died of a drug overdose at the age of 30. Much of the material arises in developing countries (especially Thailand and the Philippines) and makes use of subjects whose participation is driven by abject poverty if not outright duress.

Harmful Social Consequences

Though there has been little study of the subject, the conventional wisdom of the porn industry is that the typical customer is a reasonably educated and affluent male in his late 30s or early 40s. It's not a business that has traditionally had any interest in marketing itself to kids. That said, the video revolution has made porn available on a scale and with an ease that didn't exist when I was in school. I'm told now that at college-age parties it has become de rigeur to have a sex video playing in the background. Not long ago a Florida coed protested successfully on civil rights grounds when her university stopped her from projecting a sex tape on the side of a campus building for a party she was throwing.

The Internet makes porn imagery even more easily available, and in virtually limitless variety. It would be a miracle if kids weren't finding this stuff, even if it means going around "filters" provided by their parents or their Internet service providers. A disabling obsession with porn is already frequently categorized as a paraphilia—a fetish, like pedophilia or coprophilia or an obsession with shoes. The standard view is that whatever causes someone to displace their sexual interest on a fetish object, it typically begins in adolescence or childhood. If exposure builds up tolerance, and tolerance makes the problem worse, having unlimited porn imagery within easy reach of every computer is likely to produce social effects that we haven't yet reckoned with.

Holding back these tides might seem a losing battle, but giving up the obscenity weapon certainly hasn't helped. Obscenity laws rest on the enforceability of a certain minimum "community standard." Where that minimum might lie has become a stumbling block for prosecutors, but the courts have generally upheld the right of communities to draw some kind of a line. Up until a few years ago, despite the unquestioned profits to be made delivering hard-core porn over cable lines, fear of political and legal repercussions kept the cable companies out of the business.

If the politicians want to launch a useful debate about the corrupting influence of the mass media, the place to start is not revisiting tired and unproven accusations about Hollywood sex and violence and public morality. For one thing, they're not going to do anything about a "problem" that has been debated at least since Elvis swiveled his hips on Ed Sullivan in the 1950s. On the other hand, it would seem within the normal job description of our political leaders to discuss a genuinely new phenomenon, one with consequences that are likely to be substantial if as yet unknown, and one where their own unheralded change in law enforcement priorities has played an important role. If the universalization of access to hard-core pornography isn't worth talking about, what is?

A Constitutional Amendment Against Flag Desecration Is Justified

by Patrick Brady

About the author: *Patrick Brady is a retired army major general and chairman of the board of the Citizens Flag Alliance (CFA), a coalition of groups that believes desecration of the American flag should be illegal. Brady gave the following testimony at a 1999 House of Representatives hearing on a proposed constitutional amendment to prohibit flag desecration. As of May 2002, the CFA is still working to gain support for the amendment.*

My name is Pat Brady. I am the Chairman of the Board of the Citizens Flag Alliance. We are a coalition of some 138 organizations representing every element of our culture, some 20 million souls. We are nonpartisan and have one mission and one mission only: to return to the people the right of the people to protect their flag, a right we enjoyed since our birth, a right taken away from us by the Supreme Court. We, the people, 80% of us to include the 49 states who have petitioned congress and 70% of that Congress, want that right back.

But our concerns are not sentimental, they are not about the soiling of a colored fabric, they are about the soiling of the fiber of America. We share with the majority a sincere anxiety that our most serious problems are morally based, and that morality, values and patriotism, which are inseparable, are eroding. This erosion has serious practical consequences. We see it in sexual license, crimes against our neighbors, our land, in our failure to vote, our reluctance to serve and in the level of disrespect we have for our elected officials.

And we see a most visible sign in the decline of patriotism in the legalized desecration of the symbol of patriotism, our flag. Because it is the single symbol of our values, our hope for unity and our respect for each other, the legalized desecration of Old Glory is a major domino in the devaluing of America.

Excerpted from Patrick Brady's testimony before the House of Representatives Committee on the Judiciary, Subcommittee on the Constitution, March 23, 1999.

Patriotism and Respect for the American Flag

Supreme Court Justice John Harlan spoke about the connection between patriotism and flag desecration when he said, "love both of the common country and the state will diminish in proportion as respect for the flag is weakened." And there can be no doubt that respect for the flag has weakened. And that is tragic because when love of the country is diminished, so is our country.

Respect for our flag has, throughout our history, inspired the values that our patriots died for, values that make us the most respected nation on earth. Those values are vital and inspirational to our children, and to our future. Old Glory is the greatest training aid we have to instill patriotism in our children.

A patriot is one who loves, supports and serves his country. A patriot will take their love to the highest level—to sacrifice. Their love is the very foundation for the security and prosperity of this country. But we must be a lovable people, if we are to be worthy of sacrifice. Are we? Many gave their lives for the country they served, how many would give their lives again for the country we are becoming?

And this is the most serious danger of becoming a less lovable, a less inspirational, a less patriotic country, that it will result in the spawning of generations who will not care for their country, who will refuse to serve or to sacrifice for America, no matter how legitimate and imminent the threat. And who will encourage the same behavior in their children.

Military weakness will guarantee war and defeat. Moral weakness will guarantee the defeat of democracy. Burning the American flag is the sign of moral weakness in an individual. To legalize the burning of the American flag is the sign of moral weakness in America. When we have lost the symbol of our liberty, how long will it be before we lose the substance of our liberty?

Although our concerns are practical, the flag certainly evokes a sentimental response from many of us. It is a constant reminder of the horrors suffered by so many to bring us the bounty that is America. But it was adopted for practical purposes, it was the glue between the Declaration and the Constitution, it unified 13 very diverse and disparate colonies. It marked our place among the nations of the world. It was the trademark of freedom. Sentiment aside, its greatest worth is practical. The flag ignited the fire in the hearts of our patriots, burning the flag will put that fire out.

> *"The legalized desecration of Old Glory is a major domino in the devaluing of America."*

I think it is important that when we speak of values, we are speaking to and for our children. Nothing that is said in this debate will change adults or our values, it is too late for us. We are done. It is the children who are forming their values that are important.

The highest form of patriotism is service to our youth. The flag is the greatest training aid we have to teach our children patriotism, respect and citizenship.

[Author] Pearl Buck, in describing the treasures that are our children, tells how the flag is such a precious symbol to children and so important to their development. The greatest tragedy in flag mutilation is the disrespect it teaches our children, disrespect for the values it embodies, and disrespect to those who have sacrificed for those values. How can we teach our children respect when they are free to burn the symbol of respect? Disrespect is the genesis of hate, it provokes the dissolution of our unity, a unity which has only one symbol—the flag.

Flag Burning Is Not Speech

We are not here to change the Constitution, we are here to reclaim, to restore the Constitution. We would never do anything to harm the Constitution. Most patriots have not done a lot of speaking and writing about the Constitution, but they have done a lot of working and fighting for it. They are the source of all the freedoms in the Constitution, in fact, of much of the freedoms throughout the world.

It is not the media who gave us freedom of the press. Our patriots did. It is not the ACLU who gave us freedom of speech. Our patriots did. It is not the campus demonstrators, burning our flag, who contribute to peace. It is the men and women who served and sacrificed under the flag, and who respect the values it embodies, who are our real peace demonstrators. They

> *"The greatest tragedy in flag mutilation is the disrespect it teaches our children."*

have demonstrated for peace by contributing to our strength which is the very essence of peace.

They see no threat to any freedom in their efforts to recapture their flag, rather they see the threat in the defilement of the symbol of freedom. They all understand the right to free speech, and would die for that right, what they do not understand is that defecating on the flag is speech.

Speech is the persuading power that moves people to the ballot box, and those elected to the will of the people. Flag burning is the persuading power of the mobs. One should not be allowed to substitute hateful, violent acts, for rational, reasonable speech, to be heard. That is the last resort of those who cannot properly articulate their cause but seek power at any cost. It is certainly cowardice, and terrorism, to take one's venom out on helpless individuals or objects who cannot defend themselves. And it is moral cowardice to ignore such acts.

Flag burning is not speech, it is conduct and neither conduct nor expressive conduct are in the First Amendment. We are strengthened in this conviction by the members of five Supreme Courts in this century who have defended the right of the people to protect their flag. But the greatest authority is the men who framed the First Amendment and adopted the first flag, Thomas Jefferson and James Madison. These great Americans denounced flag burning as an assault on our sovereignty, a crime, and not in any way speech.

We are amazed at those who say the flag symbolizes the freedom to burn it. Who could seriously believe that anyone died so that the flag could be burned? Our patriots did not give so much of body and soul, on the battlefields of this century, to keep the likes of [dictators] Hitler, Kim Il Sing and Ho Chi Minh from dishonoring our flag, to see it dishonored on the streets of America.

> *"Where in the Constitution does it say that toleration for conduct that the majority sees as evil is necessary for our freedom?"*

The beauty of the flag amendment is that it does not change the Constitution. It simply takes the control of the flag away from the courts, who have ruled that defecation on the flag is "speech," and returns that control to the people where it resided since our birth. This amendment restores the Constitution to where it was before the Court amended it in 1989. Another beauty of this amendment, for those who want a statute, is that once the people regain control of the flag it can then be protected only by congressional statute.

Ironically, the only path to a statute is by way of the flag amendment. And that statute will then be subject to congressional vote and presidential veto.

Critics of the Flag Amendment

We wonder why some express fear of a slippery slope, that this amendment, if passed, will lead to many more amendments. Why should doing something right cause us to do something wrong? And what is wrong with amending the Constitution if that is the will of the people? The courts have been amending the Constitution for years according to their will without regard to the will of the people.

The people take their responsibilities to the Constitution very seriously. There have been some 11,000 attempts to amend the Constitution. The people have allowed it to happen only 27 times. And in every instance that the people amended the Constitution, it has been improved. The First Amendment, women's voting and the abolition of slavery are examples.

We have a proven record of the non-effect of flag protection on freedom.

We are offended by those who say our effort represents a tyranny of the majority. They would have us believe that a super majority of the people, the states and the Congress are ethically inferior to a small minority who oppose this amendment. The true danger to America is that a minority who were raised on a different playing field than the rest of us, most of whom never saw a battlefield, will exercise a tyranny over an indifferent and apathetic majority.

Our veterans spent much of their lives in confrontations with a minority who thought they knew better than the majority what was best. Far too often they forced their will on the majority. In Berlin where a minority build a wall around the majority and then shot those who tried to climb it. In Korea where a minority has enslaved the majority and forced the people to treat them as deities. And in Vietnam where a minority killed millions after we failed to protect them. All of us saw what Hitler and a minority did to Germany and the world.

The founding fathers foresaw the dangers of a tyranny of the minority and that is why they put the amendment clause in the Constitution, to insure that its ownership did not pass to a minority in the courts or the Congress. Thomas Jefferson said, "I readily suppose my opinion is wrong, when opposed by the majority." And, "It is my principle that the will of the majority should always prevail. . ."

The wisdom and morality of the majority is the source of democracy and our protection against tyranny.

We are convinced that our laws should reflect our values. Where in the Constitution does it say that toleration for conduct that the majority sees as evil is necessary for our freedom? Toleration for evil will fill our society with evil. Even those who oppose a flag amendment profess to be offended by flag desecration. Why tolerate it? What possible connection does toleration of evil have to the Constitution and our freedom?

We are dismayed at the insensitivity of those who would trivialize this issue. Many tell their constituents that flag burning is rare, only a handful since 1989. That is not true, there have been hundreds. Over 300 in one cemetery alone. In my state they have flag sitters to protect flags from the coffins of loved ones which are flown on patriotic holidays. This is a most cynical argument. What has the frequency of an event have to do with whether it is right or wrong? It doesn't happen often that the President is threatened, or someone jokes about bombs on an airplane, or shouts fire in a theater, or kills a bald eagle, but these things are wrong and should be unlawful—and they are.

To those who say we are trying to make felons of flag burners, not true. If it were up to me I would handle it as a ticket. Send them to class and attempt to teach them how vital respect is in a society as diverse as we are. Forty-seven states still have statutes against flag desecration and in 40 of those states, flag desecration is only a misdemeanor offense. The Congress, when it establishes a flag desecration law of the land, will certainly follow the rule of the majority of the States.

Protect Old Glory

The flag protection amendment is a perfect example of democracy at work. It is the majority in America exercising their right to rule, to demonstrate who is in charge here. The Supreme Court, a minority, by one vote, forced the American people, the majority, to accept flag desecration. Those who want the right to protect their flag are not trying to force the minority to accept flag protection, or even to respect the flag. We are trying to force the government to let the people decide, to take the flag out of the hands of a minority and give it back to the majority who can then protect it if they will.

The Constitution gives us the right to peacefully protest an action of the nation. That is what we are doing. It does not give us the right to violently protest the foundation of the nation. That is what the flag burners are doing.

We agree with the President who said that Francis Scott Key's Star Spangled Banner was a treasure and asked all Americans to save it for the ages. We are asking the same for all Star Spangled Banners.

There are great and gifted Americans on both sides of this issue. And learned opinions, but only one fact—the American people want their flag rights returned. Whatever concerns some may have, I pray they will muster the courage to believe that this once they may be wrong, and the American public may be right. I hope they will have the compassion to defer to those great blood donors to our freedom, many whose final earthly embrace was in the folds of Old Glory.

Restrictions Against Hate Speech Are Necessary

by Michael Israel

About the author: *Michael Israel is director of the criminal justice program at Kean University.*

Virtually every case that the courts see regarding the First Amendment involves symbolic speech such as lettering on garments and offensive offhand utterances. Not since *Terminiello v. Chicago* (1949) has a speech itself been tested. That case involved conditions of a speech as a Communist riot outside a hall threatened to disrupt a speech by a neofascist.

However, on November 30, 1993, at Kean College in New Jersey, Khalid Muhammad, a spokesman for the Nation of Islam, left behind a 3-hour audio tape that has strained the First Amendment in a manner that may portend the future.

"I came to pin the tail on the honky," introduced his baleful excursion of hatred toward Jews, all Whites, Catholics, the handicapped—especially the blind and those in wheelchairs, homosexuals, and nearly all Blacks who were not exactly like him. He literally praised Hitler, and he blamed the victims for the holocaust. He called for the mass murder of all Whites in South Africa. Jews received his greatest venom because purportedly they are the "blood-suckers" of the ghettos via their control of the White House, Congress, the Federal Reserve Board. They hold just about all power in America. Jews, Whites, and homosexuals are "all in the same group together." All Jews, because they killed Christ, are "from the synagogue of Satan," and they are "the devil."

This was an unadorned hate speech that was premised on the biological and genetic superiority of the Black race, "the chosen people." The speech left me numb. Of course, it has been defended by First Amendment declaration about the right to hear controversial views, which has deflected evaluation of its content.

Reportedly Muhammad had given this same speech many times on campuses and elsewhere; however, this particular speech became highly politicized. A verbatim transcript was published in *The New York Times* and, subsequently,

Excerpted from "Hate Speech and the First Amendment," by Michael Israel, *Journal of Contemporary Criminal Justice*, February 1999. Copyright © 1999 by the *Journal of Contemporary Criminal Justice*. Reprinted with permission.

many politicians denounced it. Even the U.S. Senate voted 97-0 to condemn the speech's hate dogma. Louis Farrakhan, the leader of the Nation of Islam, although refusing to disavow it, eventually dismissed Khalid Muhammad from his leadership position.

Any constitutional doctrine that claims that it protects Nazis, White supremacists, pornographers, gangster rappers, TV violence, gratuitous films, a rogue's gallery of deviants and exploiters, and very few others, and now Black racists, is going to have to justify itself, both in law and in politics. To survive it will have to be rethought and, perhaps, redefined to be preserved in some form.

Traditional Views of Speech

The First Amendment ("Congress shall make no law . . . abridging the freedom of speech, or of the press . . .") is clearly at the core of modern American democracy. However, there is a major difference between free speech and other procedural issues—such as criminal law or civil rights—that regulate the relationship between the citizen and the state. No clear line separates good from evil. If there is a right to speak (there is not always, but if there is), that right protects hate speech as well as unpopular but provocative political views.

The criminal law is often seen as the struggle between good and evil, but traditional definitions of free speech recognize no such boundary. Criminal law regulates behavior or conduct—the *actus reus* of crime—and speech, even symbolic speech, has traditionally been seen as lacking an overt act and, therefore, does not complete the material elements of a crime.

Traditional theories of the First Amendment have tended to protect any form of expression from government regulation that does not cause or threaten immediate bodily harm. The element of harm that comes from free speech can be reduced to an amoral equivalency: Nazis are protected the same as holocaust survivors, the Ku Klux Klan has the same legal footing as those who favor civil rights.

> *"Words can harm, especially to [groups such as] African Americans, abused women, Nazi death camp survivors and their descendants, and homosexuals."*

A Supreme Court justice once defended obscenity with a legendary, "No woman has ever been raped by a book." This reflects the most traditional approach to free speech. It has sometimes been called the laissez-faire theory in which the state should not interfere with any expression short of criminal solicitation to harm, or a clear and present danger to overthrow the government or at least incite a riot. In other words, being offended is not a sufficient harm to justify legal intervention.

Still, in an emerging multicultural America, a growing literature and case law has been arguing that words can harm, especially to people who have been persecuted in the past, like African Americans, abused women, Nazi death camp survivors and their descendants, and homosexuals (who often bear the worst brunt of it).

A growing literature argues that if the criminal law exists to protect innocent people from intentional injury, then victims of historic injustices may not have further indignities laid on them in the name of free speech. The 21st century may not again see a new Third Reich; however, there is no doubt that we will have to deal with a new set of atrocities. Klan nightriders will become daylight marchers. How to deal with whatever threatens humanity will not only be challenged militarily and by the criminal law, but also by the First Amendment as well. History has told us that disorder often begins with words about disorder.

There is a trend to reject free speech as a sacred ideal. According to this thinking, free speech is merely an abstraction that has gained its meaning from the uses to which it has been put, and those with political power have defined its limits for their time and place. Because there has never been absolute free speech, those in power (or on the bench) have always disallowed speech of a kind they disliked.

An example of this realistic approach may be illustrated in the area of pornography. University of Michigan Law Professor and militant feminist Catharine MacKinnon connects a world full of abused females to a flourishing pornography industry. Although explicit sex has never enjoyed complete First Amendment protection, the vagueness of its contours

> *"The Constitution . . . should protect only those forms of speech or expression that contribute to [democratic government]."*

has effectively created a laissez-faire sexual marketplace with wares ranging from hard core explicitness to network television's prurient exploitation.

Her attack on the marketplace has two thrusts, both of which may be transferable to other issues. For one, she warns without data that pornography may induce males to act out their fantasies, and women are always the victims. In other words, speech may not only be an outlet to expend one's fantasies, but also some people may actually try it out. That would be the overt act the criminal law contemplates.

Also, she argues that some uncensored language intrinsically degrades females. For example, sexual harassment represents words that are understood as acts; however, they are arguably protected by the First Amendment. These attacks raise an old jurisprudential question: What is the value of a legal system or Constitutional right that ignores the sufferings of its victims to preserve the logical purity of an abstract principle? Harassment has little substantive value to defend.

The same question arose in the early 1980s in Skokie, Illinois, when American Nazis wearing swastikas won in court the right to march through a town populated largely with elderly holocaust survivors. This is the consequence of a free speech theory that sees government censorship as the only evil from which to be guarded. We are seeing an outcry that other evils must be taken into account in any appraisal of the limits of free speech.

The Purpose of the First Amendment

The origins of the First Amendment were forged in politics as well as philosophy, and any belief in a given meaning that is explicit in its language and history should be seriously questioned. Some new thinking has applied old standards from the original Constitution itself and its primary architect, James Madison. According to this view, the main purpose of the Constitution is self-government, and any First Amendment question should ask what kinds of expression will contribute to a government by discussion and by those willing and able to discuss. Thus, a cross fertilization of ideas should produce wise policy.

The Constitution, then, should protect only those forms of speech or expression that contribute to that democratic end. This would put the content of speech on more than one level, with political speech enjoying the highest level of protection. Only toward this speech should the laissez-faire approach apply. The 1919 dissent of Justice Oliver Wendell Holmes would pertain only to political speech: "The ultimate good desired is better reached by free trade in ideas—that the best test of truth is the power of the thought to get itself accepted in the competition of the market" (*Abrams v. United States*).

In dealing with this theory of a free marketplace of ideas, the test of what the First Amendment protects would be Madisonian, which sees democracy as a government by open discussion. Does this communication contribute to a social order in which the sovereign people are free and able to engage in the kinds of deliberative debate necessary to attain our democratic goals? Freedom of speech, then, is not a good unto itself, but an instrument to pursue truth.

The rarest form of speech to fall under First Amendment jurisprudence is the public speech itself, but it has a tendency to fall under the premise of protection. Modern America is fraught with many other forms of expression, such as offhand utterances, arm bands, garments, epithets, signs, and the like. "Fighting words" would have lesser protection, and they might be subject to regulation. Such venting is where an emerging concept called *assaultive speech* can consider the hurtful consequence of speech combined with a liberty interest in expression.

This new law would consider not only the hurtful consequences, but also the category of speech. Just as there are two tiers to speech content—political speech having the highest protection, and fighting words the lowest protection—the Supreme Court has begun to articulate two tiers of harms caused by assaultive speech. Some harms have a Constitutional protection of their own grounded in the Equal Protection Clause of the Fourteenth Amendment.

According to this view, as hate speech humiliates and degrades members of historically subjugated groups, it treats them as less than full human beings, which violates their Fourteenth Amendment rights to equal protection of the law.

In a conflict of Constitutional rights, equality takes primacy over liberty, especially when the liberty is symbolic speech and deserving of less than full protection.

An African American family that had just moved into a White neighborhood in St. Paul, Minnesota, awoke in the night to see a cross burning on their lawn. When the conviction of a juvenile violating a cross burning statute was challenged, six justices argued that the city would be justified in a "judgment that harms based on race, color, creed, religion, or gender (Fourteenth Amendment grounds) are more pressing public concerns than the harms caused by other fighting words" (*R.A.V. v. St. Paul*, 1992).

> *"Hate speech humiliates and degrades members of historically subjugated groups."*

A Georgia law that prohibited the Klan from wearing a mask in public was upheld as being content neutral (not aimed at any particular group), and related to a substantial governmental interest. Although defended as symbolic speech, hood wearing was seen as having a history of creating fear and menace, even though it is not immediately intimidating *(State v. Miller,* 1990).

There is precedent then for speech regulation that protects a politically neutral governmental interest. That means a statute regulating speech would not be overturned on First Amendment grounds if it protected all groups based on race, religion, or the like and if it attempted to regulate expression that has a history of intimidation and fear that denies victims their full humanity, like the burning cross and the Klan hood.

Precedents for Restricting Speech

The standard for a test of First Amendment rights can be traced to Justice Oliver Wendell Holmes's classic opinion in the 1919 case, *Schenck v. United States,* that tested an Espionage Act passed by Congress 2 years before. More than 2,000 persons were prosecuted under the act and nearly half convicted for "uttering . . . disloyal, profane, scurrilous, or abusive language . . . intended to cause contempt, scorn, contumely, or disrepute" against the government. In point of fact, Schenck was opposing the World War I draft, but Holmes equated that with "falsely shouting fire in a theater, and causing a panic." He then set out a legal test that arguably exists to this day:

> The question in every case is whether the words are used in such circumstances and are of such a nature as to create a clear and present danger that they will bring about the substantive evils that Congress has a right to prevent." (*Schenck v. United States,* 1919)

The standard in 1919 was extremely restrictive. Schenck was distributing a leaflet that proclaimed, "A conscript is little more than a convict." His conviction and sentence of 6 months in jail was affirmed because the Court gave great weight to "the substantive evil that Congress has a right to prevent."

Compare that substantive evil with a 1993 leaflet distributed by Tom Metzger, leader of the White Aryan Resistance:

> In the waging of a guerilla war on the American continent . . . we have free physical access to small arms and ammunition . . . where a Jew or an ally of the Jew is found, and they can be easily recognized by their class distinctive activities and possessions, he will be dispatched.
>
> This harassing of the enemy will break down almost completely the structure by which the enemy rules the country. The last phase of the operation will be the use of heavy weapons against the enemy's citadels and residences. We will be in no hurry to negotiate with him in light of his treacherous nature. . . . Military victory is required.

Tom Metzger has been successfully sued for the civil rights violation of encouraging the skinhead-beating death of a Black student; however, he engaged in recruiting and organizing in addition to his speech. His manifesto calling for a new holocaust presumptively falls under First Amendment protection. The substantive evil issue lacks a definition. The definiton ought not be whatever or whomever those in power dislike; however, dispatching all Jews, although not an imminent likelihood, has a history of intimidation and fear not unlike the burning cross and Klan hood.

The liberty interest has had many articulate spokespersons, and perhaps there is no better statement than Justice William O. Douglas's 1949 majority opinion in *Terminiello v. Chicago.*

> A function of free speech under our system of government is to invite dispute. It may indeed serve its high purpose when it induces a condition of unrest, creates dissatisfaction with conditions as they are, or even stirs people to anger. Speech is often provocative and challenging. It may strike at prejudices and preconceptions and have profound unsettling effects as it presses for acceptance of an idea. That is why freedom of speech, though not absolute . . . is nevertheless protected against censorship or punishment, unless shown likely to produce a clear and present danger of a serious substantive evil that rises far above public inconvenience, annoyance or unrest. . . . There is no room under our Constitution for a more restrictive view. For the alternative would lead to standardization of ideas either by legislatures, courts, or dominant political or community groups.

Dissenters found Terminiello's speech to be fighting words that were outside First Amendment protection. Justice Felix Frankfurter wrote that the authorities were entitled to preserve the public peace "at least so long as danger to public order is not invoked in bad faith as a cover for censorship or suppression" (*Terminiello v. Chicago*, 1949).

Offensive Speech vs. Assaultive Speech

The problem is distinguishing offensive speech, as Douglas would protect in his Terminiello opinion, from assaultive speech, like cross burning and the Klan hood. It should be remembered, however, that Douglas's theory of a free marketplace of ideas has never been universally embraced by the Supreme Court or American law, and it is found in only a few majority opinions in the mid-20th century, and even those are often closely divided cases.

Still, offensiveness is clearly not a grounds for regulation. Burning the American flag is viewed as offensive by many Americans, such as war veterans for whom it is especially painful.

> *"Speech that offends should be protected; speech that assaults should not."*

Yet flag burning was held to be protected free speech when a political demonstrator in 1984 at the Republican National Convention in Dallas doused a flag with kerosene and set it afire as a crowd chanted "America, the red, white, and blue, we spit on you!" (*Texas v. Johnson*, 1989).

The Supreme Court held that burning the flag was expressive conduct, and wrote,

> If there is a bedrock principle underlying the First Amendment, it is that the Government may not prohibit the expression of an idea simply because society finds the idea itself offensive or disagreeable. (*Texas v. Johnson*, 1989)

Society indeed did find the idea offensive and disagreeable. The U.S. Senate immediately passed a law prohibiting flag desecration by punishing anyone who "knowingly mutilates, defaces, defiles, burns . . . or tramples" on the flag. At the same time the president called for a Constitutional amendment.

Flags were burned protesting that law on the U.S. Capitol steps. In 1990, the Supreme Court struck down the federal law as well, finding "It suppresses expression out of concern for its likely communicative impact" (*United States v. Eichman*, 1990; *United States v. Haggerty*, 1990).

The government argued that a recent national consensus favored punishing flag burners. The Court wrote, "Any suggestion that the government's interest in suppressing speech becomes more weighty as popular opposition to that speech grows is foreign to the First Amendment."

However, there still may be a useful difference between unpopular political speech ("America . . . we spit on you"), and racist, assaultive speech that has no discussive value, like the Nazi march through Skokie, or Khalid Muhammad at Kean College calling Jews bloodsuckers. The opinion lingers that an absolute First Amendment defense of hate speech glorifies racism that conflicts with a substantial Fourteenth Amendment governmental interest, and the cost is not borne by the community, but is a "psychic tax imposed on those least able to pay."

Of course, psychological harm is difficult to define; however, the position of Matsuda and other critical race theorists is that harm is an argument that they ought to be able to make. African Americans who have faced bigotry, holocaust survivors who have seen the marching swastikas, gays who have faced the taunts, they are all unlikely to see psychological harm as undefinable.

What is needed is a clear, content-neutral standard that rejects the equivalence of all speech. The standard must distinguish Madisonian political speech that contributes to rational discourse from gratuitous hate speech that causes harm and subverts legitimate governmental interests toward both self-government and equal protection under the law. Speech that offends should be protected; speech that assaults should not. The Klan and the National Association for the Advancement of Colored People are not equivalent. Nor are Nazis and holocaust survivors. Not if we believe in self-government in a multicultural America.

What "not protected" means has a complexity of its own but, briefly, there are three sanctions that are available to limit speech: criminal charges, tort (a civil suit), or, simply, to deny a forum. The first two mean that a particular expression ought never to be allowed; the third simply means that it is not allowed here. Furthermore, the first two can only apply to speech already given, but the latter can be of speech not yet given.

Ordinarily, prior restraint is abhorrent to First Amendment principles. It is reserved for only the rarest and most dangerous of expressions, and an injunction toward a clear and present danger of a serious threat is filed. The concept of assaultive speech is for a danger that is psychological and spiritual—hardly the kind that fits traditional prior restraint categories. Yet, if the sanction is so mild as to merely make a statement, "not here and now," there is no chilling effect, no serious stifling of debate, no loss of self-government by discussion. However, the government has escaped moral relativism (equivalency) that has historically been seen as the precursor to fascism.

Five Criteria to Define Hate Speech

A problem remains: How do we recognize hate speech when we see it? It must never be speech we simply do not like. It must be speech that assaults, speech that "by its very utterance causes injury" (*Chaplinsky v. New Hampshire*, 1942).

Five criteria need to be evaluated, with the burden on the government to convincingly argue that all five have been met to remove First Amendment protection. According to a reasonable person (Criterion 1), does the dominant theme of the material, taken as a whole (Criterion 2), cause injury (Criterion 3) without redeeming social value (Criterion 4) under the current facts and circumstances (Criterion 5)? Let us take them one at a time.

Criterion 1. The reasonable person criterion is ambiguous, but is generally understood in criminal law. The jury may become the reasonable person, in other words, the conscience of the community. Judges are experienced in evaluating material, like criminal intent, as an abstraction like any reasonable person would. The standard could be applied to hate speech, but we cannot let our most sensitive or self-interested community members do it. First Amendment jurisprudence can apply the reasonableness standard to ascertain the intent of the utterance, and its harm.

Louis Farrakhan claims his speeches are about empowerment, but Jews and Whites are frequent targets of his oratory which is clearly emotional, anti-intellectual, and scapegoating. White supremacists claim their intent is White pride, but they appear to require at least a symbolic victimization to achieve that pride. The factual question that a jury may have to determine about a given presumed hate speech is whether the plethora of negative references is expressive or gratuitous.

> "An absolute First Amendment puts victims of assaultive speech in a no-win position."

Criterion 2. When evaluating a speech we have to look at the whole speech to find the dominant theme—taken as a whole—and not judge a large amount of material by a few remarks. An offhand remark or an epithet away from the lecture hall would stand a considerably lesser chance of First Amendment protection.

Because the remedy is a prior restraint (albeit temporary), the focus is not directly on a speech but on a speaker, and what has been said in the past. Rev. Jesse Jackson has made objectionable remarks about Jews, but these were exceptions to his oratory and clearly, taking his material as a whole, he is not a hate speaker. On the other hand, Khalid Muhammad is reported to have spoken 22 minutes straight about blowing up gas stations and yanking Whites out of cars at stoplights.

Criterion 3. The injury must clearly go beyond being offensive, unpopular, or unsettling. The material must cross the line into realms of the criminal law of assault, and it must stigmatize, persecute, or degrade. There must be an identifiable victimized group or individual. If the victim is put in fear, it need not be imminent, but it must be attached to a history of intimidation like the Klan or the holocaust.

This has been called a "tort of outrage," and is an emerging jurisprudence that may become the legal signature of the 21st century in areas of human relations. This issue compels us to rethink what free speech is. After the utterance, the speaker usually moves on and does not have to deal with the consequences. The definition of harm is where the boundaries of responsible liberty come into focus.

The harm inflicted by hate speech is real and long lasting, according to Charles Lawrence of Stanford University Law School: "Psychic injury is . . . being struck in the face, and is often far more severe . . . (and) often causes deep emotional scarring, and feelings of anxiety and fear that pervade every aspect of a victim's life" (p. 24). "The experience of being called 'nigger,' 'spic,' 'Jap,' or 'kike' is like receiving a slap in the face." Lawrence cites symptoms ranging from rapid pulse rate and difficulty in breathing to nightmares, post-traumatic stress disorder, psychosis, and suicide.

Criterion 4. Even if the dominant theme of assaultive material psychically injures a reasonable person, it still may deserve First Amendment protection if there is a concurrent redeeming social value. Here again, the government-by-discussion standard applies. The censor must argue that there is nothing of discussive value in the content.

Assaultive speech functions as a "preemptive strike," says Professor Lawrence, and is experienced like a blow—not a preferred idea—and once the blow is struck a dialogue is unlikely to follow.

A traditional argument in defense of violent extremist speech is that the hostile motives are expended by expressing it. That is, saying it substitutes for doing it and, therefore, speech is a release and contributes to social control. There is no legal doctrine supporting this expend theory, and social science currently leans to the opposite. "Disorder leads to more disorder" is more the current thinking, and hate speech contributes to anomie. Eventually the physical assaults that hate speech memorializes will take place. Although limits to free speech should be viewed with suspicion, the absence of limits may be more perilous.

Because the consequences of free speech are hard to measure (and probably no clear social control theory emerges), we have little choice but to evaluate the content, and to assume that the utterance is an act unto itself; therefore, an *actus reus* exists in words.

After Khalid Muhammad's Kean College speech and the storm of publicity it invoked, the apparent result was an escalation of his rhetoric. After an intense politicized period during which Farrakhan approved of the content, Muhammad, in a February 19, 1994, speech in Baltimore, intensified his tirade against Jews as the killers of Christ, and prayed that "God will kill my enemy."

Criterion 5. Current facts and circumstances may protect some material, but if those circumstances change, the First Amendment protection changes. The fighting words doctrine was borne during World War II when the epithet "God damned fascist" was successfully prosecuted *(Chaplinsky v. New Hampshire,* 1942). Today the same insult would have little impact.

Here is where the substantial governmental interest concept is applied. A hate speech on a college campus—an institution with a mission that is the opposite of hate speech—may be considered a substantive evil that the government (the college administration) has a right to prohibit. In a different setting (such as a homogeneous community), that same speech may bring no harm. If the remedy is merely denial of a forum, then facts and circumstances become a much more relevant standard because an imminent riot is not the required harm.

If a public college contemplating the return of a hate speaker, or a town like Skokie facing a Nazi march, could determine (under those circumstances, according to a reasonable person, and taking the dominant theme of the material) that there is harm beyond offensiveness without redeeming social value, then First Amendment protection could be withheld. The burden would then be on the speaker or marcher to possibly take court action, and if the speaker could successfully attack any one of the five standards, he would be entitled to First

Amendment protections under traditional standards (i.e., unless imminent threat of riot). The weight must always fall on the government when it limits speech, and it must make the case with all the presumptions favoring the expressive individual. Yet, regulation has both legal precedent and an emerging compelling interest. A future jurisprudence must take into account victims.

Free Speech Needs Boundaries

The marketplace has become a poor regulator. When a speech issue becomes politicized there is no intellectual free trade, but an intense competition of sound bites and phrases calculated to catch the attention of a bored public emerges. The press has an appetite for "the other side."

Small fringe groups like the Nation of Islam or the White Aryan Resistance can make an outrageous assaultive statement, and the press legitimates it by seeking a counter opinion. We are reduced to absurd specious issues—the degree of Jewish involvement in the slave trade, or the native intelligence of the Black race—where there is no meaningful equivalency of opinion.

An absolute First Amendment puts victims of assaultive speech in a no-win position. When the hateful speech is given, to not respond leaves it uncontradicted, and responding gives it legitimacy—a viewpoint worthy of debate.

The traditional liberal view of the First Amendment believes that the good speech will drive out the bad speech—the marketplace will regulate—but the good speech reaches different audiences, and hate speech becomes "the other side." That is the ultimate moral harm. A First Amendment that does not adjust to the new American reality will be in danger of being nothing more than symbolic. What passes for participatory self-government will become a battle of the streets—which speaker gets the bigger crowd and the bigger press—without any relevant discussion. Free speech will continue to be the sanctuary of charlatans who use it in utter cynicism to protect themselves from criticism. What we all want is real free speech, but relevant freedom needs boundaries. The criminal justice system sets limits on free behavior. It will have to address limits on free speech as well.

Censorship of Violence in Popular Entertainment Is Not Justified

by Judith Levine

About the author: *Judith Levine is a journalist, essayist, and the coauthor of* Harmful to Minors: The Perils of Protecting Children from Sex. *The following viewpoint is excerpted from* Shooting the Messenger: Why Censorship Won't Stop Violence, *a report that Levine prepared for the Media Coalition, a free speech advocacy group.*

In May 1999, shortly after the Littleton, Colorado, murders, a North Carolina high-school student typed the words "The end is near" on a computer screen as a joke about millennial madness. Another student saw the message, called it a threat, and the school agreed. The boy was expelled for a year, then arrested. After three nights in jail, he was found guilty in state court. His original 45-day jail sentence was suspended, but he was penalized with 18 months of probation and 48 hours of community service. A 13-year-old student in Texas fulfilled an assignment to write a "scary story." His story mentioned the shooting of real people. He was arrested and jailed for six days. In the Denver area, schools banned black trench coats, because the Columbine shooters and their friends were known to wear them. These excessive sentences and overreactions to teenagers' behavior not only violate the Constitutional rights of minors, they also contribute to kids' disaffection from school and the law. As child protection, they are useless, and may even be counterproductive.

An Old Issue

In the late 19th century Anthony Comstock, chief special agent of the New York Society for the Suppression of Vice, pored over innumerable moral "traps for the young" that were a staple of middle-class households—half-dime novels, "story papers" and even the daily newspapers. The New York Society for the Prevention of Cruelty to Children "kept a watchful eye upon the so-called Museums of the City," whose advertisements were "like magnets to curious children." According to one society report, a play featuring "depravity, stabbing, shooting, and blood-shedding" so traumatized a 10-year-old girl that she was found "wander[ing] aimlessly along Eighth Avenue as if incapable of ridding herself of the dread impressions that had filled her young mind." In a 1914 issue of *The Atlantic*, Agnes Repellier, a popular conservative essayist, inveighed against the film and publishing industries "coining money" by creating a generation sophisticated in sin. She may have been the first essayist to propose a governmentally run rating system, asking "the authorities" to bar minors "from all shows dealing with prostitution." (Today that category would include films like *Pretty Woman* and *Trading Places*.) In the 1920s and '30s, jazz came under attack, in the '50s, comic books were regulated, and in the 1960s, rock and roll was decried as a source of the evil that produced everything from premarital sex to resistance to the Vietnam war.

Today, these examples seem prudish, quaint, or simply wrong. What is outrageous in one era is ho-hum in another. But the generation gap has been around for at least two centuries. Since there has been anything resembling youth culture, adults have been exercised about its forms of expression. Frank Sinatra called Elvis Presley's music "the most brutal, ugly, desperate, vicious form of expression it has been my misfortune to hear," and "the martial music of every . . . delinquent on the face of the earth." Today's generation of parents blamed heavy metal and rap music for young people's suicide and alienation in the 1980s; video games, Internet chat rooms, raves and other aspects of youth culture have all come under fire in the '90s. As technology gallops forward, with kids confidently at the reins, adult technophobia has become outrage. Adults often attempt to censor, not only what kids see and hear, but increasingly, what they say and create.

Advocates of censorship say that shielding children from certain words and images protects them. In fact, it can endanger them. For instance, Internet filtering software installed in the computers of New York City's public schools has blocked students' access to Web sites about breast cancer, child labor, anorexia and safe sex. High-school students cannot call up information about diabetes among

> *"When people want to censor material they find vile or violent or disturbing, it's as if they think all the emotions that give rise to the interest in [those materials] will go away."*

black and Hispanic teens because the relevant sites mention erectile dysfunction. Such "protection" will only diminish kids' ability to keep themselves healthy and to participate intelligently in a complex world.

A student of Henry Jenkins at MIT who had been a goth for many years described what that identity, with its black clothes and taste for macabre music, meant to her. "In high school, before there was even the label goth, some of the disenfranchised youth started to hang out together to give ourselves a safe place to be depressed.

The Benefits of Free Expression

People want a safe space to explore the more depressing aspects of the world they live in. They don't want to feel guilty for not being happy all the time, they don't want to be told to get on Prozac, and they don't want to force themselves to put on masks for the benefit of the people around them." The journal of Columbine shooter Eric Harris opened with the sentence: "I hate the fucking world." He also hated, among numerous other people and things, slow drivers in the fast lane, the WB network, Tiger Woods, and, if his suicide is a clue, himself. Did The Cure or Nine Inch Nails make those goths depressed? Did a neo-Nazi Web site teach Harris to hate everybody? Will prohibiting sales of CDs or blocking

> *"Whatever you think of what kids are watching, listening to or saying, they have a Constitutional right to it."*

Internet sites to minors cheer up unhappy kids, or turn a boy like Eric Harris into a peacemaker? "When people want to censor material that they find vile or violent or disturbing, it's as if they think all the emotions that give rise to the interest in [those materials] will go away," said David Sanjek, director of the BMI Archives and a former educator. A lot of what attracts kids to horror movies or hostile lyrics, he said, is "trying to deal with issues of power" central to growing up and making it in school. "A child isn't going to give up his desire to destroy what has power over him if you don't let him go see a Freddy Krueger movie," Sanjek added.

A rap song about a murder is not a murder, a heavy metal song about suicide is not self-annihilation. The cross-dressing Marilyn Manson is not a seducer. When he snarls at the Church, he's not burning a cross. As MIT's Henry Jenkins told Congress, kids know that pop culture performers are putting on an act, playing a part—a part that offers a sublimated outlet for the audience's anger at authority or ambivalence about sexuality or organized religion. Similarly, no killing is going on in the killing rooms of Doom. The video game instead gives kids a play space to work out fantasies of destruction without destroying anything but pixels on a screen.

In more literal ways, video games can be therapeutic. Psychologists have taken advantage of the state of "relaxed alertness" induced by games to treat attention deficit disorder, depression and anxiety and to rehabilitate people with brain injuries. And they're educational. Video games hone logic and coordination skills. Players commonly achieve the highly pleasurable combination of deep concentration and intellectual mastery called "flow." That, plus the motivation to win, puts players in an optimal frame of mind for learning—anything from the Highway Code for drivers to safe-sex negotiation. In fact, video gaming is positively associated with higher IQs: Kids with higher scores play video games more.

Censorship Is Not the Answer

Prohibition turned out to be one of the biggest social-policy mistakes of the 20th century. The popular demand for liquor created a booming black market. This gave the burgeoning American Mafia a leg up in business, created a wave of violent crime and made every social drinker a criminal. Especially because the evidence is so weak that violent content in the media presents a danger to kids, crackdowns on access may do children more harm than good. Do we really want them to have to break the law to see a movie with violent content like a classic John Wayne movie or Schindler's List? Some critics have suggested that such enforcement might only fuel the trade in fake identification, and other forms of subterfuge. It could also backfire in another way. Said one 14-year-old interviewed by *The New York Times*, "If you put more restrictions on [a movie], kids will just want to go even more."

"Minors are entitled to a significant measure of First Amendment protection, and only in relatively narrow and well-defined circumstances may government bar public dissemination of protected material to them," observed the Supreme Court in 1957. This is still true." Whatever you think of what kids are watching, listening to or saying, they have a Constitutional right to it. And curtailing anyone's rights threatens everyone's rights.

Censorship of Sex-Related Speech Violates the First Amendment

by Marilyn C. Mazur

About the author: *Marilyn C. Mazur is an attorney for the National Coalition Against Censorship, an alliance of nonprofit organizations that promotes freedom of expression.*

Are [photographer] Jock Sturges' photographs of nude children on the beach child pornography? Does learning about sex or reading about homosexuality cause young people to experiment with sex in ways they otherwise wouldn't? Should children be shielded from nudity in art and sex on the Internet? Can words like "masturbation" and "contraception" be banned from classroom discussions? Should parents always have the final say about what minors can read, see, and learn?

These are the issues at the center of many of the censorship wars in late 20th century America. In one sense, it's part of our tradition. From the ban on [birth control pioneer] Margaret Sanger's use of the words syphilis and gonorrhea to the ban on [authors] James Joyce and Henry Miller, the censors have traditionally focused on sex. The debate has shifted, however. While First Amendment protection now extends to a great deal of material with sexual content—at least for adults—where children are concerned, all bets are off. As a result, most censorship wars over sex are now fought ostensibly to protect minors, and to define what is "harmful to minors."

Parents are understandably and rightly concerned about their children's sexual decisions and behavior. For some parents, sex is something reserved only for adults, limited to certain circumstances and relationships. Other adults and children have different values, goals and expectations. One rule plainly does not fit all, so how are questions about what kind of information about sex is harmful—or essential—to minors to be resolved?

Noted children's author Judy Blume has observed that "children are inexperienced, but they are not innocent." Children live in a world in which sex education is censored, but sex is glamorized in advertisements and on television, and the sexual activities of government officials are described in the morning papers and the evening news. Sexually transmitted diseases and unwanted pregnancy are other realities familiar to many teenagers. In the absence of empirical evidence demonstrating harm, perhaps it is time to reconsider whether it is constitutional—or wise—to deny young people access to information they need to make informed decisions and appropriate choices.

Sex, Sexuality, and the Law

All but the most astute legal scholars are confused. What is the legal definition of obscenity? How is it different from pornography? What is child pornography? What is the meaning of terms like "harmful to minors," and which images are considered "indecent"?

The laws regulating material with sexual content have become increasingly complex, but sex is by no means a new subject in censorship law. Americans are heir to a tradition, fostered by religious perspectives, that viewed sex as something to be tolerated, at best—a necessary evil. In the 19th century, Anthony Comstock, founder of the New York Society for the Suppression of Vice, campaigned on the slogan "Morals, Not Art and Literature" for censorship laws to suppress erotic subject matter in art and literature and information about sexuality, reproduction and birth control. The Comstock Act of 1873 banned all material found to be "lewd," "indecent," "filthy" or "obscene," including such classics as Chaucer's *Canterbury Tales*. At one time or another, books by Ernest Hemingway, D.H. Lawrence, John Steinbeck, F. Scott Fitzgerald and a host of other literary greats have been banned under obscenity laws. Legal attitudes only began to change officially in 1957, when the Supreme Court acknowledged that sex is "a great and mysterious motive force in human life."

The legal definition of *obscenity* has gone through several permutations, with its current definition embodied in the 1973 case, *Miller v. California.* Material with sexual content falls outside the protection of the First Amendment if 1) the work, taken as a whole, appeals to a prurient interest in sex, as judged by contemporary community standards, 2) it portrays sexual conduct, defined by law, in a patently offensive manner, and 3) the work lacks serious literary, artistic, political or scientific

> *"It is time to reconsider whether it is constitutional—or wise—to deny young people access to information [about sex]."*

value. *Pornography*—jokingly referred to by lawyer and author Marjorie Heins as "the dreaded P word"—is not the same as obscenity. Pornography is erotic material or material that arouses sexual desire. In contrast with obscenity, pornography enjoys First Amendment protection because it does not satisfy the

Miller standard, either because it has artistic, literary, historical or other social value, or because it is not patently offensive under community standards—even if some may find it so, or because the work taken as a whole does not appeal exclusively to a prurient interest in sex. Much of the material that is targeted as "indecent" is protected, at least for adults.

Children, however, are another story. Five years before *Miller*, the Court articulated a different standard for minors' access to sexual material. In *Ginsberg v. New York*, the Court upheld a New York statute criminalizing distribution of material deemed "harmful to minors" (under 17), reasoning:

> . . . the concept of obscenity or of unprotected matter may vary according to the group to whom the questionable material is directed. . . . Because of the State's exigent interest in preventing distribution to children of objectionable material, it can exercise its power to protect the health, safety, welfare and morals of its community by barring the distribution to children of books recognized to be suitable for adults.

Material may thus be deemed "harmful to minors" if it appeals to the "prurient, shameful or morbid" interest of minors, lacks serious social value for minors, and is "patently offensive" based on adult views of what is fit for minors. This "variable obscenity" standard has been faulted because it upholds "unlawful to minors" laws without requiring the government to prove a compelling state interest or actual harm. It arguably applies equally to an emancipated 16 year old and a 4 year old child.

Ginsberg limited minors' access to material with sexual content, but that is not the end of the story. In *New York v. Ferber*, the Court also upheld restrictions on various *depictions* of minors that are or could be considered sexual. The Court recognized the potential overbreadth of the statute—which could apply not only to child pornography, but also to a *National Geographic* photographic essay on tribal rites, ancient Greek art, and textbooks showing the effects of child sexual abuse or genital mutilation—but upheld it, citing the compelling need to protect actual children from possible exploitation by child pornographers. Left open was the question whether material apparently prohibited under the statute would be protected if it had literary, historical, scientific, or artistic value. That question remains unanswered, but since then the Court has demonstrated continued concern about possible exploitation of children used to create sexual materials, and upheld a law criminalizing an adult's *possession* of child pornography in his own home.

These issues are in the forefront of a current debate over the Child Pornography Protection Act of 1996. The CPPA criminalizes not only sexual images involving actual children, but also computer-generated images, the use of "body doubles," and sexual images that appear to be minors, or that are advertised as minors, even if no minors are actually involved. Thus far, however, the statute has fared relatively well in the few courts to consider it. One federal district court found it unconstitutionally vague and overbroad, in a decision reversed on appeal, and another upheld the statute on the theory that such materials facilitate sexual exploitation of children. The CPPA signals a significant shift. A computer-generated image of a minor portrayed in a sexual manner is not the same as a picture of an actual child, and raises wholly different concerns from those expressed by the Court in *Ferber* and *Osborne*—the protection of real children from possible exploitation. The CPPA represents an unprecedented effort to suppress the ability to explore the *idea* of minors as sexual actors through pictures, film and theater. Without a recognition that the First Amendment protects such materials if they have artistic, historical, scientific, literary or other value, the CPPA could influence how *Romeo and Juliet* is presented, chill display of art like Balthus' *The Guitar Lesson*, and discourage exhibits of ancient and contemporary erotic art and statuary. It has already affected U.S. distribution of a 1997 film version of *Lolita*, and emboldened authorities in Oklahoma to seize the film of Gunter Grass' classic World War II novel, *The Tin Drum.*

The notion of "variable obscenity," and the Court's willingness to alter the terms of First Amendment analysis in cases involving minors as observers and objects in art and literature with sexual themes also helps explain *Federal Communications Commission v. Pacifica*, where the Court upheld an FCC broadcast rule banning "indecent" speech or "patently offensive depictions or descriptions of sexual or excretory activities or organs," except on supposedly child-free "safe harbor" late night hours. The FCC's action against Pacifica Radio targeted comedian George Carlin's "Filthy Words" monologue, whose clearly satiric nature was apparently lost on the FCC and the Supreme Court, much as the anti-Nazi message of *The Tin Drum* was lost on the police in Oklahoma City.

> *"Pornography enjoys First Amendment protection."*

Although the Supreme Court has generally endorsed increasingly restrictive laws wherever children and sex were combined, last year it refused to apply the *Pacifica* child-protective rationale to sex on the Internet. In *Reno v. ACLU*, the Court struck down the Communications Decency Act which targeted "indecent" speech on-line. Granting cyberspace the highest level of First Amendment protection, the Court also took the occasion to comment on the positive social value of sexually explicit speech, declaring that terms like "indecent" and "patently offensive" are so broad and vague as to threaten "serious discussion about birth control practices," homosexuality, prison rape, or safer sex in addition to "artistic images that include nude subjects" and "arguably the card catalogue of the Carnegie Library." Perhaps this represents a turning point in the Court's willingness to scrutinize more closely claims about "harm to minors," and to evaluate more seriously their independent need for access to materials with sexual content.

The uncertainty may be resolved soon. In October 1998, Congress enacted the Child Online Protection Act, also called "CDA II" because it is a successor to the Communications Decency Act. It would prohibit material deemed "harmful to minors" on commercial sites on the Internet. The President signed the bill, notwithstanding the fact that the United States Department of Justice expressed reservations about its constitutionality. Almost immediately, the law was challenged on the ground that it violates the First Amendment, as applied by the Supreme Court in *Reno v. ACLU*; the federal district court hearing the challenge has so far agreed that it is constitutionally suspect. [On May 13, 2002, the Supreme Court partly upheld the Child Online Protection Act, ruling that it is not unconstitutional to use "community standards" to define what is harmful to children. Other challenges to the law are still before the courts.]

Sex Education

What if I want to have sex before I get married?

Well, I guess you'll just have to be prepared to die. And you'll probably take with you your spouse and one or more of your children.

Students are best motivated to delay sex when they are provided with full and accurate information about conception, contraception, safe sex and emotional and psychological aspects of sexuality and reproduction, according to a persuasive body of social science research. There is no persuasive support for the proposition that sex education encourages sexual experimentation or increased sexual activity. The American Psychological Association has reported that comprehensive sex education, that also provides students with behavioral strategies to avoid sex, can be successful in delaying sex and avoiding teen pregnancy. In fact, most teens are sexually active. The Commission on Adolescent Sexual Health estimates that 50% of females and 75% of males ages 15 to 19 have had sexual intercourse. These teenagers need reliable information on how to protect themselves from pregnancy, AIDS and other sexually transmitted diseases: an estimated 3 million teens—about one in four who are sexually active—acquire a sexually transmitted disease every year.

Despite this, in 1996 Senators Lauch Faircloth (R-NC) and Rick Santorum (R-PA), with the help of right wing groups like the Heritage Foundation, quietly attached a section entitled "Separate Program for Abstinence Education" to the Personal Responsibility and Work Opportunity Reconciliation Act of 1996, which overhauled welfare. The provision, buried at the end of the 250-page bill, provides $50 million a year for 5 years to states for abstinence education. The law specifies that funded programs, among other things, must teach: 1) the social, psychological and health gains of abstinence; 2) that abstinence is the only way to avoid pregnancy and sexually transmitted diseases; 3) that a mutually faithful monogamous relationship in the context of marriage is the expected standard of human sexual activity; 4) that sex outside marriage is likely to have harmful effects and that out-of-wedlock pregnancy is harmful to the child, the parents and society.

This legislation requires funded programs to censor information on contraception and disease prevention to promote an abstinence message. Curricular materials for such programs include *Sex Respect, Facing Reality*, and *Teen Aid*. All use scare tactics to convey the message that pre-marital sex is dangerous and immoral; all are homophobic in endorsing sex in marriage as the only acceptable expression of human sexuality; they also rely on gender stereotypes and contain medical misinformation. The National Coalition for Abstinence Education, under the aegis of Focus on the Family, distributes widely a "report card" which grades state plans strictly on their adherence to the tenets of the federal abstinence program, disregarding all else.

> *"The fear-based approach to sex education has spawned old-fashioned censorship incidents."*

Some communities have fought against this form of censorship and viewpoint discrimination. Shreveport, Louisiana, successfully challenged the use of *Sex Respect* and *Facing Reality* on the grounds that they violated church-state principles and contained medically inaccurate information. Although every state has applied for funding, many are struggling to use the money without undercutting other comprehensive sex education programs, for example through programs to educate younger children or media campaigns like Michigan's "Sex Can Wait" program and Maryland's "Virgin: Teach your kid it's not a dirty word."

The fear-based approach to sex education has spawned old-fashioned censorship incidents. In Franklin County, North Carolina, the school board ordered three chapters—dealing with AIDS, sexually transmitted diseases, contraception, marriage and parenting—literally razored out of the 9th grade health textbook. The action was recommended because the book used the word "partner" instead of "spouse," and encouraged abstinence until ready for sex instead of marriage. The school health coordinator's advice was ignored: "We don't believe that knowledge of contraception is going to cause kids to go out and have sex. We believe knowledge is empowerment. It's ignorance that's a problem." Equally amazing, District 24 in Queens, New York, has had a policy for more than a dozen years to ban from the curriculum four words: masturbation, homosexuality, abortion and contraception.

The media has sometimes played an inflammatory, if contradictory, role in the debate. Bryant Gumbel's "Public Eye" program on CBS revealed its bias in the introduction to a story about a comprehensive sex education program run by the Unitarian Universalist Fellowship in Concord, Massachusetts: "Film strips that go all the way and then some . . . and you won't believe where—in a church!" The 25-year-old *voluntary* church-based program, which teens attend with parental permission, provides co-ed discussion of the biology, morality, ethics, health, risks, and mechanics of sex, guided by female and male adults. The obvious merits of such an approach, however, were ignored by a largely sensational treatment on TV—the same medium that brings "Baywatch" to many teens on a weekly basis.

Suppression of frank information about sex is also a hot topic in Hauppauge, Long Island, as a result of demands by a parent and a parish priest that the magazines *Seventeen, YM* and *Teen* be removed from middle school library shelves. The superintendent says the magazines are not "age appropriate," and endorsed their removal because they don't teach "abstinence as the best way to prevent AIDS." The magazines contain articles on peer pressure, divorce and conformity, along with factual columns about sex, bodies and health—they are also the number one place girls get information about sex and their bodies. Censorship of this sort is not confined to the lower grades. Last year, administrators at the State University at New Paltz came under fire for authorizing a women's study conference that dealt with repression of female sexuality as an aspect of repression of women, and included topics on sado masochism, lesbianism and other sexual topics. And Nassau Community College has been locked in a court battle for years with critics of its *elective* sex education course, who complain that the course "advocates an anti-religious sexual ethic" and violates the Establishment Clause of the First Amendment.

Partly as a result of the assault on comprehensive sex education, only 3 percent of teenagers learn about sex from sex education classes, according to a recent poll. That figure is down from 18 percent in 1986. That statistic may well drop to zero in the future, if politicians, the media, judges, and educators continue to insist that denying teens information about sex will reduce their interest in it.

Gay and Lesbian Themes

The proponents of abstinence-only and fear-based sex education programs are predictably hostile to the idea and practice of homosexuality. The same evangelical groups that have challenged comprehensive sex education have waged an aggressive campaign to purge public schools of books about gays and lesbians, to deprive students of information about gay/lesbian sexuality, and to deny public funding for arts and cultural programs with gay and lesbian themes.

The Manhattan Theater Club in New York City recently garnered criticism when it caved in to pressure from the Catholic League for Religious and Civil Rights, and withdrew a planned production of Terrence McNally's play *Corpus Christi* depicting a gay Christ-like figure. The MTC ultimately reversed its position, after a public outcry. However, in 1997, San Antonio eliminated funding for the Esperanza Center for Peace and Justice, a national leader in combining cultural arts programming with a broad range of social justice advocacy, because of its sponsorship of a gay and lesbian film festival. Cobbs County, Georgia and Mecklenburg County, North Carolina have also eliminated local arts agencies completely rather than support works with homosexual characters or themes. Similarly, Out North Contemporary Art House in Anchorage, Alaska, whose director is an openly gay man, lost funding because its presentations are not "mainstream" shows "you would take your own family to."

Public funding for the arts is not the only target of censorship efforts focussing on gay and lesbian themes. The Idaho Board of Education recently denied funding for a research project about gay communities. In Jefferson County, in Louisville, Kentucky, three novels by openly gay author E. Lynn Harris were pulled from the shelves of Central High School when two parents complained. Commented the English teacher who had the books in her classroom, "If you ban these books, you subtract role models from these students who have all too few." A nationwide campaign against two books, *Heather Has Two Mommies* and *Daddy's Roommate* has been fought by conservative groups saying they promote homosexuality. In North Carolina, Hertford County school officials destroyed a gay-themed book and 2,000 others deemed "inappropriate." Just last month, free concerts by famed folk-rock group, the Indigo Girls, were canceled at high schools in South Carolina and Tennessee, in part because the Grammy Award winning singers are lesbians.

Many of these actions reflect the success achieved by pro-censorship forces in getting elected to school and library boards and local arts organizations. As these events reveal, such a strategy can be highly effective, but it is not foolproof so long as there are parents and students willing to fight for their own First Amendment rights. For example, in 1996 a federal judge in Kansas ruled that *Annie on My Mind*, a book about two girls who fall in love and struggle with declaring their homosexuality, could not be removed from the school library because school officials disapproved of its content.

The Internet is the latest and hottest arena for censorship debates about the issue of sexual orientation. There is intense pressure to block and filter minors' access to sexual content on the Internet, and gay and lesbian sites are a particular target. In response, gay advocacy groups complain that although many gay Internet sites are about culture and identity and not sexual behavior, all information that touches on gay themes is rendered invisible. Thus, a gay square dancing site or a gay resource directory, sites that do not contain sexually explicit material, will be blocked. In an ironic turn-

> *"There is intense pressure to block and filter minors' access to sexual content on the Internet, and gay and lesbian sites are a particular target."*

about, the American Family Association website was recently blocked by Cyber Patrol, because of intolerance towards gays and lesbians.

Depriving minors of information about various forms of sexual expression is troublesome on many fronts—ranging from concerns for their physical health, emotional well-being, and intellectual growth and freedom to inquire about life in all its aspects. It is especially tragic, however, if it also contributes to the gay youth suicide rate, which is three times higher than that of non-gay youths.

Chapter 1

Nude Art and Other Dangers

Nudity—frontal or otherwise—involving sexual activity or otherwise has always offended a certain number of people. But shifting standards of what is acceptable for family viewing and of what is "harmful to minors" has lowered the threshold so that today it seems as if the body itself has become taboo. Nudity has been sexualized.

Frontal nudity is not tantamount to obscenity. Indeed, in much classic art, the nude form is neither erotic nor offensive. Nonetheless, distribution of pictures depicting nudity *could* be considered illegal under a variety of existing statutes and standards. Child pornography statutes have been used to target artists whose work involves children, and even parents who take pictures of their own children.

In a recent well-publicized case, prosecutors charged Barnes & Noble with violating state law by displaying Jock Sturges books with photographs of nude children where minors could see them. Sturges, an award-winning photographer whose work is in the Museum of Modern Art, the Metropolitan Museum of Art and the Bibliotheque National of Paris, has been targeted by Focus on the Family and Loyal Opposition, headed by Randall Terry, former leader of the anti-abortion group Operation Rescue and currently running for Congress. Some of the charges against Barnes & Noble have been dropped, after it agreed to display Sturges books higher than five and a half feet, while others are still pending. Other less visible cases have turned an innocent picture taking session into a nightmare, like that experienced by a Wayne State University art professor, who was investigated for child abuse when a janitor found a nude photograph of her three year old child in her wastebasket.

Books and photographs are not the only focus of such attacks. The Academy-Award winning film, *The Tin Drum*, was seized from the Oklahoma City library, private homes and video stores because of complaints by Oklahomans for Children and Families. The film's message, about the disintegration of central Europe during the rise of Naziism, was completely overlooked by OCAF in its attack on a few isolated and suggestive, but not explicit, scenes. [In 1998 a federal court ruled that the film was not child pornography and that the state's seizure of copies of the film was illegal.]

Another artistic casualty of the sex and censorship wars is the 1997 film version of *Lolita*, starring Jeremy Irons. True to the Nabokov novel, the film explores a man's sexual obsession with a prepubescent but precocious girl, and uses a body double in sexually explicit scenes. Although the film has been shown in Europe, *Lolita* [had difficulty finding] a distributor in the U.S., undoubtedly because of uncertainty about whether it will elicit charges of child pornography.

What of *National Geographic* pictures of naked children involved in tribal rituals? Medical textbooks displaying children's genitals? Scholarly description of children's sexual fantasies? Could these be construed to violate state pornography statutes which prohibit "lascivious exhibition of genitalia"? That questions like these exist is enough to predict a chilling effect on scholarly writing and distribution of such materials. The ambiguity of the legal standards, the absence of any limiting principle that protects work with artistic, scholarly or other merit, and vagueness about what is harmful to minors all plainly contribute to censorship.

> *"Sometimes efforts to protect minors from nudity and sexual knowledge verge on the ludicrous."*

Most problematic is the idea that children shouldn't see a depiction of a naked body. Consider the decision by one TV station to cancel an educational film teaching women breast self-examination techniques because the broadcaster decided the material was "inappropriate for family viewing." This was the same theory on which the New York State Museum recently asked sculptor Kim Waale to remove portions of her work, *A Good Look: The Adolescent Bedroom Project*. Similarly, many libraries have "no nudes" policies for their public exhibit space, resulting in the exclusion of Robin Bellospirito's highly stylized nudes. Tulane student artist Jenny Root's nude sculpture, *Mother/Father*, was moved so it wouldn't accidentally be seen by children. The aversion to artistic representations of the human body recently reached new heights at Brigham Young University, where four sculptures of nudes, including *The Kiss*, were removed from a traveling Rodin exhibit. Bellospirito won her right to exhibit her paintings in court; Waale and two other artists withdrew their work from the New York State Museum in protest, but art lovers in Utah who hoped to see *The Kiss* were out of luck.

Sometimes efforts to protect minors from nudity and sexual knowledge verge on the ludicrous. On Long Island, an edition of *Where's Waldo?*, the charming mini figure puzzle book, was banned because hidden among hundreds of tiny figures crammed onto the "beach" page someone found a woman with a partially exposed breast the size of a pencil tip. In Erie, Pennsylvania, teachers used markers to block out passages of mating habits from naturalist Diane Fossey's *Gorillas in the Mist*. In New York, a teacher was disciplined for allowing other students to read a composition about a sexual experience written by a fellow student. Octorara, Pennsylvania, school officials removed a Margaret Atwood story, "Rape Fantasies," from the high school honors English curriculum.

Nudity is opposed on both sides of the ideological spectrum. Goya's famous *Nude Maja* hung on a classroom wall for 15 years until a professor charged that it was "sexually harassing." In New York City new zoning rules will exile to remote areas most sex shops, topless clubs, and bookstores featuring sexually explicit but constitutionally-protected fare. The language of the ordinance is broad enough to apply not only to "peep shows," but also to a smash hit like *Oh! Calcutta!* or an art gallery specializing in nude art; it was recently declared constitutional by a federal appeals court.

While the religious right is fueling much of the effort to ban these materials from our communities, the religious community is by no means monolithic in its views. Consider the exuberant Sister Wendy who charmed millions with her TV programs on the history of art including many nude and sexually explicit works. Consider, too, the highly touted sex education programs embraced by religious people and organizations, including American Baptists and the Unitarian Universalists. Morality is not the province of the far right, and repression of information about sex and sexuality and of images of nudity in art is not universally accepted as correct by all religions.

Censorship Is Counterproductive

Public health experts repeatedly confirm the value of comprehensive sex education, which ironically appears to decrease minor's interest in pornography. High school students with access to condoms, and knowledge about how to use them, do not engage in more sex, but use protection more often when they do. Again and again, we learn that gay and lesbian youth need information and role models to survive physically and emotionally. Denying young people timely access to the information they will need as adults is both cruel and counter-productive.

By relaxing the standards for judging censorship where minors and sex are involved, the courts have invited some of the disarray now apparent in sex education, community access to art, and minors' access to information about sex, health and the body. . . . Until the courts begin to scrutinize the question of "harm" more closely, students may miss out on an important part of the education they need to prepare for life; artists and art lovers will continue to experience the chill of uncertainty; and the entire community will remain vulnerable to those who charge that protection of minors requires a fig leaf on Michaelangelo's *David*, a bikini on Matisse's *Blue Nude*, sex education courses that don't talk about sex, and a closet large enough to hold the entire gay and lesbian community.

A Constitutional Amendment Against Flag Desecration Would Undermine the First Amendment

by Kenneth A. Paulson

About the author: *Kenneth A. Paulson is senior vice president of the First Amendment Center, a nonprofit organization that advocates freedom of the press and freedom of speech.*

It was a classic American moment: the San Francisco Giants on the field, the national anthem on the public address system—and one jerk on his cell phone.

While thousands around him doffed their hats and turned to the flag before the game began, this man, who appeared to be in his mid-30s, kept both his baseball cap and his cell phone on, oblivious to the ceremony.

He also was oblivious to the angry reactions of those around him. Fans glared at him, and at the close of the song, several muttered about the lack of respect. But no epithets were tossed or punches thrown. These were polite patriots. One man said, "This guy deserves to have his ass kicked," but then apologized to other fans for his language.

I was a little surprised at just how irritated I was. I found myself hoping for a line drive off the man's head.

If one guy with a cell phone can stir so much emotion at a recent ballgame, it's little wonder that terrorist attacks on New York and Washington have led to a new wave of patriotism all across the United States. This, in turn, has fueled a well-intentioned but destructive movement to bar flag burning by passing a constitutional amendment.

At first glance, most Americans are inclined to provide constitutional protection for the national symbol. The very notion that people would burn a flag—even if it's their own flag on their own property—is bothersome.

The History of Flag Desecration

Still, it would surprise most Americans to note the Founding Fathers were not particularly concerned with protecting the flag. In fact, as detailed in Robert Justin Goldstein's excellent book, *Saving Old Glory*, the U.S. flag was not a particularly important symbol for the first 75 years of the nation's existence. It wasn't until the Civil War that the flag—symbolizing the Union—came to have real sentimental value for Americans.

Further, the first efforts to prevent flag desecration had nothing to do with flag burning. The original concept was to prevent the tacky use of the American flag in advertising. We all know how well that's turned out.

In time, flag-desecration laws were applied to people who burned flags to protest U.S. government policy. People were imprisoned for burning flags; one young man was even jailed for wearing a flag patch on the seat of his pants.

In 1989, and again in 1990, the U.S. Supreme Court found that burning a U.S. flag in protest was in fact an exercise of free speech. This decision made legal sense. It also made common sense.

After all, when someone burns an American flag, they're conveying a political message that you couldn't duplicate by burning a bath towel. And the only motive for punishing the burning of one's own private property is to silence an opinion you find unpalatable.

Normally, a Supreme Court decision puts an end to litigation and maneuvering. After all, there's no higher court to which you can direct your appeal.

The only option left to veterans groups, who felt strongly that the flag needed protection—even if it meant changing the very fiber of the U.S. Constitution—was to spend more than $15 million lobbying Congress for an amendment.

From the beginning, voting for an amendment was politically irresistible. Members of the House of Representatives—subject to re-election every two years—have always voted for it in overwhelming numbers. In the Senate, the measure has fallen short of the two-thirds majority by a handful of votes. If it ever passes there, it will go to the states for ratification.

Over the last few years, 49 of the 50 states have already passed resolutions saying they will ratify the amendment if it is sent to them. The sole holdout was Vermont, a state

> *"The U.S. Supreme Court found that burning a U.S. flag ... [is] an exercise of free speech. This decision made legal sense. It also made common sense."*

with an independent streak and a real understanding of the risk of tampering with the Constitution to prevent a dozen or so people from burning their own U.S. flags each year.

For years, the political equation stayed the same. The House supported the amendment, the Senate was within a few votes of approving it, and the states were ready to hop on the bandwagon.

Curtailing Freedom

[In 2000] something remarkable happened. Some thoughtful leaders at both ends of the political spectrum recognized that "protecting" the flag would harm the Constitution. For the first time in the history of this country, we would be subtracting a freedom from the Bill of Rights.

Throughout the history of this nation, amendments have been used to give greater freedom: to give equal protection to all citizens; to give the vote to women and 18-year-olds.

The most flagrant example of denying liberty through an amendment came with the passage of Prohibition. In short order, a new amendment had to be passed to repeal it. Simply put, amendments should preserve the power of the people and not curtail freedom.

In announcing his objection to the proposed constitutional amendment, Sen. Robert Byrd, D-W.Va., may have said it best: "The flag is a symbol of the republic, the symbol of what the Constitution provides. It is not the flag that provides it. It is the Constitution of the United States. It is that Constitution that provides us with the rights that all Americans enjoy, regardless of race, regardless of color, regardless of national origin, regardless of sex. It isn't the flag."

For a time, it appeared that the flag-desecration controversy would disappear. The move to take free-expression rights away from Americans was losing steam, and it was time to move on.

Then came the tragic events of Sept. 11, 2001. Suddenly the effort to rewrite the Constitution gained new momentum.

Vermont—the one state to stand against the tide—passed a resolution supporting congressional protection of the flag. As Jack Hoffman of *The Rutland Herald* reported, "the Legislature resisted this national campaign for a long time, but after the terrorist attacks of Sept. 11, that resistance crumbled."

[In spring 2002] the Citizens Flag Alliance, a coalition of groups supporting the flag-desecration amendment, issued the results of a new opinion poll: 49% of those surveyed said they valued the flag more since the terrorist attacks of Sept. 11. The alliance contended that three out of four Americans want the Senate to approve the flag amendment and reported—somewhat ominously—that half of those surveyed said that the flag issue alone would lead them to vote against any senator who opposed the amendment.

It's easy to understand the emotional appeal of a flag-desecration amendment, particularly at this time. Still, I'm not sure that the survey asked all the right questions. The next time they go into the field, I suggest the following:

• Do you think an appropriate response to an unpopular Supreme Court decision is to change the U.S. Constitution?

- If so, what other parts of the Bill of Rights should we consider revoking? The right to bear arms? The right to privacy? What about reproductive freedom? After all, each of those rights depends upon controversial federal court or Supreme Court rulings. With just a few more amendments, we can erase a number of unpopular decisions.
- After we ban flag burning, what other objects should be protected? Surely the Bible shouldn't be burned or torn. What about the Book of Mormon? The Quran?

Changing the U.S. Constitution to prevent someone from burning his own flag would compel everyone in this country to respect the Stars and Stripes. If we're ready to take that step, then we should also make mandatory the singing of the national anthem and the reciting of the Pledge of Allegiance.

And while we're at it, we need to haul off anybody who uses a cell phone at a ballgame during "The Star-Spangled Banner."

That kind of strategy—exemplified by the flag-desecration amendment—would ensure the protection of our most treasured symbols of freedom.

In the end, though, we would have the symbols and lose the freedom.

Restrictions Against Hate Speech Violate the First Amendment

by Paul McMasters

About the author: *Paul McMasters is the First Amendment ombudsman for the Freedom Forum, an advocacy organization dedicated to free press and free speech.*

More than one year has passed, and we have yet to shake the image of Matthew Shepard pistol-whipped and strung up to die on a Wyoming rail fence because he was gay [the murder occurred on October 7, 1998]. We still shudder over the horror of James Byrd chained to a pickup truck and dragged to his death along a Texas country road because he was black. We cringe when reminded of the racist rampage of Benjamin Smith that left two people dead and nine others wounded.

America, we like to feel, has room for everyone. It is a place of tolerance, equality, and justice. Hate is a singular affront to that vision, and the lengthening list of these atrocities haunts the national conscience and quickens the search for remedy.

It once seemed easier to ignore the haters among us. They held furtive meetings in out-of-the-way places, wrote racist screeds in the guise of bad novels, and when they appeared in public, they wore hoods to hide their faces. Now, they apply for admission to the bar, stand for elected office, appear on radio and television talk shows, and increasingly take their message to the mainstream by using the Internet.

Hate has been a presence on the Internet since its inception. That presence increased dramatically with the advent of the World Wide Web. Now such sites, professionally produced and graphically appealing, number in the hundreds. More go up every day. Activists have moved quickly to confront the haters on this virtual ground, using the Internet to give the lie to hate speech, to monitor hate groups, and to highlight the problems of hate.

Thus, the Internet is forcing us to plumb the true depth of hate in our society. Because the role the Internet will play in the matter of hate is still evolving, the question arises: Will the Internet prove to be an instrument of hate, a palliative to hate, or just a shift in venue? The answer will depend in large measure on the nature of the solutions to hate that we pursue.

Hate Speech

Among the proposals advanced are restrictions on hate speech. Generally, hate speech is that which offends, threatens, or insults groups based on race, color, religion, national origin, gender, sexual orientation, disability, or a number of other traits. Proposals to restrict such speech have considerable support among victim groups, civil rights activists, scholars, political figures, and ordinary citizens. The arguments for restrictions on hate speech, whether on the Internet or elsewhere, are straightforward:

- Words can and do harm the targets of hate in painfully real ways.
- Hate speech silences the members of victim groups and denies them their rightful standing in society.
- There already are exceptions to First Amendment protections for other types of speech; surely hate speech can be added to that list.
- When it comes to hate speech, civil rights must trump civil liberties.

The calls for restrictions include declaring hate-mongers mentally ill, government monitoring of groups and individuals espousing hate, outright censorship of hate speech on the Internet, and punishment of hate speech in all forms and media. It has even been proposed that recent hate outrages justify lifting the restraints placed on the Hoover-era Federal Bureau of Investigation to allow the agency to investigate groups and individuals for religious or political speech it deems extreme.

Most Americans want to do something about the hate. In the aftermath of the October 1998 beating death of Matthew Shepard, the University of Wyoming student targeted because he was gay, 26 states took up legislative proposals dealing with hate crimes. Missouri passed such a law, and California Governor Gray Davis recently signed a bill that outlaws harassment of gays in state schools.

Hate Speech in the Courts

It is a uniquely American characteristic that such matters become the stuff of passionate debate rather than bloody warfare—remarkable considering the seriousness and divisiveness of the issues raised. When laws target speech, whether on the Internet or in other venues, profound questions are raised. Do group sensibilities take precedence over individual conscience? Is some speech so odious and hurtful that it can be regarded as conduct? Must the achievement of a civil society be at the expense of a free society?

However we eventually resolve such questions, the debate must play out in terms of what the Constitution will allow. The Supreme Court has been wary of a general proscription of hate speech. Beginning with *Cantwell v. Connecticut* 310 U.S. 296 (1940), the court set about defining and refining the conditions under which hate speech might fall outside the First Amendment's protections.

A series of these decisions—*Chaplinsky v. New Hampshire* 315 U.S.

> *"When laws target speech, whether on the Internet or in other venues, profound questions are raised."*

568 (1942), *Terminiello v. Chicago* 337 U.S. 1 (1949), *Feiner v. New York* 340 U.S. 315 (1951), and *Brandenburg v. Ohio* 395 U.S. 444 (1969)—have added such terms as "clear and present danger," "fighting words," incitement to ". . . imminent lawless action," and "the heckler's veto" to the legal lexicon. Even so, no ruling has yet yielded up a "victim's veto."

With the unanimous decision in *R.A.V. v. St. Paul* 505 U.S. 377 (1992), which held that a bias-motivated criminal ordinance was invalid because it prohibited "otherwise permitted speech solely on the basis of the subjects the speech addresses," that seems even less likely today.

In addition, there are other constitutional obstacles such as the jurisprudence involving prior restraint, group libel, and the right to private conscience (an issue explored at some length by Alan Charles Kors and Harvey A. Silverglate in *The Shadow University: The Betrayal of Liberty on America's Campuses*). Nevertheless, judges and juries in state courts are listening intently to efforts to make the case against hate speech. Attempts to expand the concepts of threat or the intentional infliction of emotional distress offer hope to advocates that a constitutionally valid approach can be devised.

Even if laws that the Supreme Court would abide could be crafted, however, there is another, more difficult, problem for the advocates of such laws: They don't stop hate. That is the fundamental flaw in solutions that focus on hate-speech laws. The proponents of such laws frequently fail to disentangle three distinct issues: hate speech, hate crimes, and the silencing of victim groups. Hate causes each of these. It does not necessarily follow that hate speech causes either hate crimes or the silencing of victim groups or that anti-hate speech laws will relieve either problem. Censoring hate speech may have emotional and symbolic appeal but little if any utility as a solution.

Outside the United States, hate often manifests itself in prolonged and violent clashes between groups. International conventions and anti-hate speech laws don't seem to have had an appreciable impact on hate or the violence that it causes, however. We have had the same experience with campus speech codes in the United States. Not only have they not found much favor with the courts, but more important, hate speech and crimes on the nation's campuses have increased appreciably despite the existence of speech codes covering broad categories of speech at hundreds of colleges and universities.

In fact, women and minorities—traditional groups for whom the speech codes were enacted—often are the ones punished under them. It is instructive to note that the defendants in the early hate-speech cases were religious or political speakers. In *Cantwell* and *Chaplinsky*, they were Jehovah's Witnesses; in *Terminiello*, a Catholic priest (albeit under suspension from his bishop at the time for racist speech), and in *Feiner*, a college student appealing to blacks to revolt against racist oppression.

Defining Hate Speech

The difficulty of defining hate speech significantly complicates attempts to draft laws against hate speech. What might work for scholarly or general discourse surely would not be adequate for the formulation of laws. Is the definition in terms of what the speech reflects, such as bigotry, bias, prejudice, anger, ignorance, and fear? Or what the speech conveys: intimidation, vilification, subjugation, eradication? Does it matter whether the speech occurs in a face-to-face encounter, in an online diatribe, in a novel, in a newscast, during a classroom presentation, or as part of a political candidate's campaign? Can hate speech be defined as a list of words, or does the context of those words count? Which is more important in determining hate speech, the intent of the speaker or the reaction of the audience?

> *"To punish hate-mongers for thoughts and words instead of actions is to alter the essential nature of our social and political compact."*

Once a definition of hate speech is codified in law, the problem becomes one of determining how it is applied and to whom it is applied. Should a law proscribe certain words and thoughts for one group of Americans but allow them for oppressed groups that have appropriated the language of victimization and discrimination as a strategy for combating hate?

For hate laws to function, hate groups must be designated for special punishment of their words and views and victim groups must be designated for special consideration—a seductive prospect in light of their history of oppression. Ultimately, however, it is an inconsistent and possibly disastrous principle to embed in law, given the potential for arbitrary justice as well as a hardening of the hate lines. Further, to punish hate-mongers for thoughts and words instead of actions is to alter the essential nature of our social and political compact.

The Problem with Hate-Speech Laws

Hate-speech laws encourage appropriation of victim groups' identities by groups that until recently had not been considered oppressed. The list of such "outsider" groups is growing. For example, an Oregon law includes along with the traditional criteria such designations as political party, purchasing power, union membership, social standing, or marital status, to name a few. As this list of victim groups expands, the universe of protected speech shrinks.

Hate-speech laws can work to silence individual members of victim groups if the speech against others falls within the definition of hate speech or if individuals within the group are only allowed to represent that group in their speech. They would be prevented from criticizing or harshly characterizing members of their own group or other victim groups.

Hate-speech laws also must depend on an accurate representation of how speech works, reasonably predicting how speech will be received. If not, application of the law becomes arbitrary and capricious. For example, if inadvertent harm is a criterion of the law—and how can it not be?—then speech against hate as well as hate speech itself becomes vulnerable to punishment since inadvertent harm is inevitable. The ironic beauty of speech is that neither the speaker nor the text can control the reaction of the audience, which may vary dramatically from one hearer to another. It is safe to say that the interpretations of a particular word or string of words in a particular context amount to some multiple of the total number of individuals and groups receiving it. Language is simply too mercurial for the constraints of legal definitions.

> *"Protecting and exercising the freedom guaranteed under the First Amendment is the best way to insure the equality guaranteed under the Fourteenth Amendment."*

Laws against hate speech would obviate the benefits of such speech—and there are benefits. Hate speech uncovers the haters. It exposes the ignorance, fear, and incoherence in their views. It warns, prepares, and galvanizes the targets. It provides the police with suspects and the prosecutors with evidence in the event of a crime. It enlivens the bystanders. It demands response. And it demonstrates the strength of our commitment to the tolerance of intolerance and the primacy of freedom of expression.

Laws restricting hate speech begin with the assumption that speech is a finite commodity so that speech must be taken from one group in order to give more speech to another group. Such an assumption offends both reason and our First Amendment tradition.

Punishing speech is not the same thing as curing hate. Ultimately, anti-hate speech laws would silence the voices they would help as well as those who would help them. They would be enacted with the best of intentions and executed with the worst of results. Rather than encouraging the assimilation of the words and work of those championing a more civil society, these laws would substitute one form of silencing for another. They would divert public dialogue from a focus on a fair society to a preoccupation with censorship. They would risk exacerbating hate rather than eliminating it. They would trivialize the debate by flailing at words and symbols rather than the causes of hate and discrimination. They would lay a veneer of civility over a community seething with tension.

Even though arguments against hate-speech laws from a First Amendment perspective seem anemic and abstract in the face of hate's graphic ugliness, they must be made. Free-speech advocates cannot merely wave the First Amendment flag and walk away. They must encourage advocates for the targets of hate to speak out against bigotry and bias at every turn. They must remind them that protecting and exercising the freedom guaranteed under the First Amendment is the best way to insure the equality guaranteed under the Fourteenth Amendment.

All efforts must focus on affirming the American tradition that no problem—even hate—is so intractable that we must censor words, images, and ideas to address it. The challenge within that tradition is to achieve civility in discourse without imposing conformity in thought. The First Amendment imperative within that tradition is to defend bad words for good principles.

Restrictions Against Offensive Speech Harm Society

by Nat Hentoff

About the author: *Journalist Nat Hentoff writes frequently on free speech and other civil liberties issues. He is the author of numerous books, including* Living the Bill of Rights: How to Be an Authentic American *and* First Freedom: The Tumultuous History of Free Speech in America.

More than 6,000 New Yorkers gathered at New York City's Foley Square in November 1999 to exercise their free-speech right to protest the presence of 18 members of the Ku Klux Klan, who were there because of their right to express their views. The Klan stood in silence because the courts had denied them sound equipment.

The fiercely hostile crowd included children whose parents wanted them to share their revulsion against these racists. As the cursing and hooting rose to a crescendo, a young woman said to no one in particular, "This is America. Even those Klan members have a right to speak."

She was surrounded, kicked, spat at, and beaten over the head with American flags. Punched at least 15 times, she fell, scrambled to her feet, and escaped.

The children in that mob had learned a lesson in the limits of free speech. There were no editorials in the city's newspapers decrying the silencing of the Klan members; and only one newspaper, the *New York Times*, mentioned, in a news story, the lesson the young woman had learned.

I found this contempt for what most Americans claim—especially on the Fourth of July—to treasure alarming but not surprising.

Growing Contempt for Freedom of Speech

The First Amendment Center—part of the Freedom Forum—issued its State of the First Amendment Survey in 2000 after asking 1,001 Americans 18 years of age or older what they thought of the First Amendment guarantee of free speech. A thumping 67 percent said that public remarks that racial groups might find offensive should not be permitted. Fifty-three percent believe the press has too much freedom—a rise from the 38 percent in the survey two years ago that urged the press to be restrained.

One might expect that at least at colleges and universities—where the free exchange of ideas is the reason for their existence—free speech might be more prized than in the country at large. However, in recent years, there has been an epidemic of destruction of conservative student newspapers; they are being stolen and sometimes burned in celebratory bonfires by students of sharply opposing views. At one such college, Cornell University, I was told by a spokewoman for the administration that the marauding students were simply exercising their free-speech rights.

> *"The basic, pervasive danger to free speech is the ignorance of the populace at large concerning their own First Amendment rights."*

When I spoke at a faculty luncheon at Cornell, I noted that I had not been aware that theft and arson were integral to the right of free speech. The only response came after the luncheon, when a dean took me aside and said, "I'm glad you said that. I can't." This was a tenured professor who was afraid of being called a right-winger, a racist, or worse if she objected to the assaults on the campus's conservative newspaper.

A particularly disturbing illustration of how much the First Amendment has been diminished is what happened to the Boy Scouts after they won, in the U.S. Supreme Court, a victory for their First Amendment right of expression and association by refusing a leadership position to an assistant scoutmaster who had publicly declared himself to be homosexual.

As a result, cities have banned the Boy Scouts from various activities in schools and other public places where they had been traditionally welcome. In New York City, I reminded school chancellor Harold Levy and his staff of the Supreme Court's quotation from Alexis de Tocqueville's *Democracy in America*: "The right of association appears to be almost as inalienable in its nature as the right of personal liberty. No legislator can attack it without impairing the foundations of society."

I was not persuasive. The chancellor has prohibited the Boy Scouts from bidding on any contracts with the school system. The city's public students have learned, accordingly, that the U.S. Supreme Court can be held in contempt by New York City's chief educator.

As I unavailingly told the chancellor, the NAACP or the Urban League (both of which have connections with public schools) cannot be forced by the state to admit members of white citizens' councils to leadership positions. Nor can a disability rights organization be compelled by the state to have followers of Dr. Jack Kevorkian as leaders.

The basic, pervasive danger to free speech is the ignorance of the populace at large concerning their own First Amendment rights—and that leads to their indifference or hostility to other Americans' rights of free speech.

When asked in the First Amendment Center's survey, "To the best of your recollection, have you ever taken classes in either school or college that dealt with the First Amendment?" 47 percent said no. Moreover, a study by the National Assessment of Educational Progress revealed that 57 percent of high school seniors were unable to show a credible knowledge of American history and the Constitution, the bedrock of our freedoms.

I can attest to this ignorance, having spoken about the Bill of Rights and the rest of the Constitution in many schools, including graduate schools, around the country. It's heartening, however, that once students are told the stories of why we have the Bill of Rights and what it took to win those liberties, they become curious to learn more. It's as if they had just discovered America.

George Orwell, who knew a great deal about what happens to a country in which the state becomes the guardian of its citizens' minds, said: "If large numbers of people believe in freedom of speech, there will be freedom of speech, even if the law forbids it. But if public opinion is sluggish, inconvenient minorities will be persecuted, even if laws exist to protect them."

Suppression of Speech from Across the Political Spectrum

There is no question in my mind that American public opinion has indeed become sluggish with regard to freedom of speech. When I was in college, many of the attempts to suppress speech came from the Right. Now they also come from the Left, where political correctness has become a secular religion. But more insidious than that development is that Americans who cannot be easily categorized as being either on the Right or the Left are passive when the First Amendment is held in contempt. A glaring current example is what is happening, without vigorous public protest, to the Boy Scouts.

Thomas Baker, who is the James Madison Chair in Constitutional Law and director of the Constitutional Law Center at Drake University Law School, has pointed out in *Legal Times*: "We cannot limit the Boy Scouts' First Amendment rights without limiting everyone's First Amendment rights. For minority groups that often face discrimination from the majority, this is a constitutional guarantee worth protecting."

But how many Americans care about that guarantee?

Chapter 2

Does Separation of Church and State Threaten Religious Liberty?

Chapter Preface

Controversy over the First Amendment's guarantee of freedom of religion is as old as the Bill of Rights itself, but as law professor Stephen M. Feldman notes in his introduction to *Law & Religion: A Critical Anthology*, "The relationship between law and religion in America has become increasingly controversial since World War II." Feldman explains that the increased controversy is due in part to the increasing number of freedom of religion cases on which the Supreme Court has ruled since the end of the war. Before the 1940s, he points out, the Court did not even recognize that the First Amendment's establishment clause—"Congress shall make no law respecting an establishment of religion"—or the free exercise clause—"or prohibiting the free exercise thereof"—applied to state governments.

Of the Supreme Court's postwar rulings on the separation of church and state, one of the most contentious was the 1962 decision in *Engel v. Vitale*, in which the Court held that the daily recitation of prayer in public schools violated the establishment clause of the First Amendment. Public outcry over the decision was so great that the 1964 platform of the Republican Party called for a Christian amendment to the Constitution.

Controversy over the role of religion in public schools continued well into the 1990s, prompting President Bill Clinton in 1995 to issue advisory guidelines to every school district in the country explaining what is and what is not permissible. According to the guidelines, which were revised again in 1998, nondisruptive individual or group prayer is allowed, as is student speech about religion. However, school endorsement of any religious activity or doctrine is prohibited, as is school observance of religious holidays and leadership of prayer by a teacher or other school official. Many school administrators have praised the guidelines for helping to clarify the issue.

Each year, however, new cases show that controversies persist. In 1998, for example, Chris Niemeyer filed suit against his California high school for prohibiting him from giving a high school commencement address because he planned to mention his Christian faith in his speech. Niemeyer argued that he had an individual right to express his religious beliefs, while the school maintained that expressing those beliefs in an official school ceremony would constitute the school's endorsement of those beliefs. A federal court sided with the school, and the Supreme Court declined to hear Niemeyer's appeal.

The Niemeyer case highlights the difficulty of balancing students' free exercise of religion with schools' prohibition against endorsing religious views. The viewpoints in the following chapter further explore the controversies surrounding religious freedom and the separation of church and state.

The Constitution's Framers Did Not Intend Strict Separation of Church and State

by Matthew D. Staver

About the author: *Matthew D. Staver is founder and president of the Liberty Counsel, a religious civil liberties education and legal defense organization established to preserve religious freedom.*

This country was established upon the assumption that religion was essential to good government. On July 13, 1787, the Continental Congress enacted the Northwest Ordinance, which stated: "Religion, morality and knowledge, being necessary to good government and the happiness of mankind, schools and the means of education shall be forever encouraged." The First Amendment prohibited the federal government from establishing a religion to which the several states must pay homage. The First Amendment provided assurance that the federal government would not meddle in the affairs of religion within the sovereign states.

In modern times groups like the American Civil Liberties Union and Americans United for Separation of Church and State have attempted to create an environment wherein government and religion are adversaries. Their favorite phrase has been "separation of church and state." These groups have intoned the mantra of "separation of church and state" so long that many people believe the phrase is in the Constitution. In Proverbs Chapter 18, verse 16, the Bible says, "He who states his case first seems right until another comes to challenge him." I'm sure you have seen legal arguments on television where the prosecution argues to the jury that the defendant is guilty. Once the prosecution finishes the opening presentation, you believe that the defendant is guilty. However, after the defense attorney completes the rebuttal presentation of the evidence, you may be confused, or at least you acknowledge that the case is not clear cut.

The same is true with the phrase "separation of church and state." The ACLU and the liberal media have touted the phrase so many times that most people believe the phrase is in the Constitution. Nowhere is "separation of church and state" referenced in the Constitution. This phrase was in the former Soviet Union's Constitution, but it has never been part of the United States Constitution.

Justice Oliver Wendell Holmes once said, "It is one of the misfortunes of the law that ideas become encysted in phrases, and thereafter for a long time cease to provoke further analysis." The phrase, "separation of church and state," has become one of these misfortunes of law.

Origins of a Misunderstood Phrase

In 1947 the Supreme Court popularized Thomas Jefferson's "wall of separation between church and state." Taking the Jefferson metaphor out of context, strict separationists have often used the phrase to silence Christians and to limit any Christian influence from affecting the political system. To understand Jefferson's "wall of separation," we should return to the original context in which it was written. Jefferson himself once wrote:

> On every question of construction, [we must] carry ourselves back to the time when the constitution was adopted, recollect the spirit manifested in the debates, and instead of trying what meaning may be squeezed out of the test, or invented against it, conform to the probable one in which it was a part.

Thomas Jefferson was inaugurated as the third President on March 4, 1801. On October 7, 1801, a committee of the Danbury Baptist Association wrote a congratulatory letter to Jefferson on his election as President. Organized in 1790, the Danbury Baptist Association was an alliance of churches in Western Connecticut. The Baptists were a religious minority in the state of Connecticut where Congregationalism was the established church.

The concern of the Danbury Baptist Association is understandable once we understand the background

> *"Nowhere is [the phrase] 'separation of church and state' referenced in the Constitution."*

of church-state relations in Great Britain. The Association eschewed the kind of state sponsored enforcement of religion that had been the norm in Great Britain.

The Danbury Baptist Association committee wrote to the President stating that, "Religion is at all times and places a Matter between God and Individuals—that no man ought to suffer in Name, person or affects on account of his religious Opinions." The Danbury Baptists believed that religion was an unalienable right and they hoped that Jefferson would raise the consciousness of the people to recognize religious freedom as unalienable. However, the Danbury Baptists acknowledged that the President of the United States was not a "national Legislator" and they also understood that the "national government cannot destroy the Laws of each State." In other words, they recognized Jefferson's limited influence as the federal executive on the individual states.

Jefferson did not necessarily like receiving mail as President, but he generally endeavored to turn his responses into an opportunity to sow what he called "useful truths" and principles among the people so that the ideas might take political root. He therefore took this opportunity to explain why he as President, contrary to his predecessors, did not proclaim national days of fasting and prayer.

Jefferson's letter went through at least two drafts. Part of the first draft reads as follows:

> Believing with you that religion is a matter which lies solely between man & his god, that he owes account to none other for his faith or his worship, that legitimate powers of government reach actions only and not opinions, I contemplate with sovereign reverence that act of the whole American people which declared that their legislature should make no law respecting an establishment of religion, or prohibiting the free exercise thereof; thus building a wall of separation between church and state. Congress thus inhibited from acts respecting religion, and the Executive authorized only to execute their acts, I have refrained from prescribing even occasional performances of devotion.

Jefferson asked Levi Lincoln, the Attorney General, and Gideon Granger, the Postmaster General, to comment on his draft. In a letter to Mr. Lincoln, Jefferson stated he wanted to take the occasion to explain why he did not "proclaim national fastings & thanksgivings, as my predecessors did." He knew that the response would "give great offense to the New England clergy" and he advised Lincoln that he should suggest necessary changes.

Mr. Lincoln responded that the five New England states have always been in the habit of "observing fasts and thanksgivings in performance of proclamations from the respective Executives" and that this "custom is venerable being handed down from our ancestors." Lincoln therefore struck through the last sentence of the above quoted letter about Jefferson refraining from prescribing even occasional performances of devotion. Jefferson penned a note in the margin that this paragraph was omitted because "it might give uneasiness to some of our republican friends in the eastern states where the proclamation of thanksgivings" by their state executives is respected.

Jefferson Believed Religion Was a State Matter

To understand Jefferson's use of the wall metaphor in his letter to the Danbury Baptist Association, we must compare his other writings. On March 4, 1805, in Jefferson's Second Inaugural Address, he stated as follows:

> In matters of religion, I have considered that its free exercise is placed by the Constitution independent of the powers of the General [i.e., federal] Government. I have therefore undertaken, on no occasion, to prescribe the religious

exercises suited to it; but have left them, as the Constitution found them, under the direction and discipline of State or Church authorities acknowledged by the several religious societies.

Then on January 23, 1808, Jefferson wrote in response to a letter received by Reverend Samuel Miller, who requested him to declare a national day of thanksgiving and prayer:

> I consider the government of the United States as interdicted by the Constitution from intermeddling with religious institutions, their doctrines, discipline, or exercises. This results not only from the provisions that no law shall be made respecting the establishment or free exercise of religion [First Amendment], but from that also which reserves to the States the powers not delegated to the United States [Tenth Amendment]. Certainly no power to prescribe any religious exercise, or to assume authority in religious discipline, has been delegated to the General [i.e., federal] Government. It must then rest with the States, as far as it can be in any human authority.

> I am aware that the practice of my predecessors may be quoted. But I have every belief, that the example of State executives led to the assumption of that authority by the General Government, without due examination, which would have discovered that what might be a right in State government, was a violation of that right when assumed by another. . . . [C]ivil powers alone have been given to the President of the United States, and no authority to direct the religious exercises of his constituents.

Comparing these two responses to his actions in the state government of Virginia show the true intent of Jefferson's wall metaphor. As a member of the House of Burgesses, on May 24, 1774, Jefferson participated in drafting and enacting a resolution designating a "Day of Fasting, Humiliation, and Prayer." This resolution occurred only a few days before he wrote "A Bill for Establishing Religious Freedom." In 1779, while Jefferson was governor of Virginia, he issued a proclamation decreeing a day "of publick and solemn thanksgiving and prayer to Almighty God." In the late 1770's, as chair of the Virginia committee of Revisers, Jefferson was the chief architect of a measure entitled, "A Bill for Appointing Days of Public Fasting and Thanksgiving." Interestingly, this bill authorized the governor, or Chief Magistrate with the advice of Counsel, to designate days of thanksgiving and fasting and, required that the public be notified by proclamation. The bill also provided that "[e]very

> *"Jefferson believed . . . that the states retained the authority over matters of religion."*

minister of the gospel shall on each day so to be appointed, attend and perform divine service and preach a sermon, or discourse, suited to the occasion, in his church, on pain of forfeiting fifty pounds for every failure, not having a reasonable excuse." Though the bill was never enacted, Jefferson was its chief architect and the sponsor was none other than James Madison.

Chapter 2

Federalism and the First Amendment

So what did Jefferson mean when he used the "wall" metaphor? Jefferson undoubtedly meant that the First Amendment prohibited the federal Congress from enacting any law respecting an establishment of religion or prohibiting the free exercise thereof. As the chief executive of the federal government, the President's duty was to carry out the directives of Congress. If Congress had no authority in matters of religion, then neither did the President. Religion was clearly within the jurisdiction of the church and states. As a state legislator, Jefferson saw no problem with proclaiming days of thanksgiving and prayer, and even on one occasion prescribed a penalty to the clergy for failure to abide by these state proclamations. Jefferson believed that the Constitution created a limited government and that the states retained the authority over matters of religion not only through the First Amendment but also through the Tenth Amendment. The federal government had absolutely no jurisdiction over religion, as that matter was left where the Constitution found it, namely with the individual churches and the several states.

"The 'wall of separation between church and state' is a metaphor based on bad history."

In summary, the First Amendment says more about federalism than religious freedom. In other words, the purpose of the First Amendment was to declare that the federal government had absolutely no jurisdiction in matters of religion. It could neither establish a religion, nor prohibit the free exercise of religion. The First Amendment clearly erected a barrier between the federal government and religion on a state level. If a state chose to have no religion, or to have an established religion, the federal government had no jurisdiction one way or the other. This is what Thomas Jefferson meant by the "wall of separation." In context, the word "state" really referred to the federal government. The First Amendment did not apply to the states. It was only applicable as a restraint against the federal government. The problem arose in 1940 and then again in 1947 when the Supreme Court applied the First Amendment to the states. This turned the First Amendment on its head, and completely inverted its meaning. The First Amendment was never meant to be a restraint on state government. It was only applicable to the federal government. When the Supreme Court turned the First Amendment around 180 degrees and used Jefferson's comment in the process, it not only perverted the First Amendment, but misconstrued the intent of Jefferson's letter.

There is nothing wrong with the way Jefferson used the "wall of separation between church and state" metaphor. The problem has arisen when the Supreme Court in 1947 erroneously picked up the metaphor and attempted to construct a constitutional principle. While the metaphor understood in its proper context is useful, we might do well to heed the words of the United States Supreme Court Justice William Rehnquist:

A Bad Metaphor

The "wall of separation between church and state" is a metaphor based on bad history, a metaphor which has proved useless as a guide to judging. It should be frankly and explicitly abandoned.

Jefferson used the phrase "wall of separation between church and state" as a means of expressing his republican view that the federal or general government should not interfere with religious matters among the several states. In its proper context, the phrase represents a clear expression of state autonomy.

Accordingly, Jefferson saw no contradiction in authoring a religious proclamation to be used by state officials and refusing to issue similar religious proclamations as president of the United States. His wall had less to do with the separation of church and all civil government than with the separation of federal and state governments.

The "wall of separation between church and state" phrase as understood by Jefferson was never meant to exclude people of faith from influencing and shaping government. Jefferson would be shocked to learn that his letter has been used as a weapon against religion. He would never countenance such shabby and distorted use of history.

Prohibiting School Prayer Threatens Religious Liberty

by Laurel MacLeod

About the author: *Laurel MacLeod is director of legislation and public policy for Concerned Women for America, a conservative public policy organization.*

In 1962, the United States Supreme Court ruled that it was unconstitutional for the state of New York to allow the recitation of prayer in its public schools. The prayer that had been read daily said: "Almighty God, we acknowledge our dependence upon Thee, and we beg Thy blessings upon us, our parents, our teachers, and our country."

Since that ruling, many facets of American cultural life have changed dramatically. Concerned Women for America (CWA) recognizes that the issue of school prayer has continued to arise because, in too many instances, *religious expression* has been denied to students. Prayer does, of necessity, carry religious connotations. The prayer issue has become a fundamental question of whether or not religious expression, in the form of prayer, is appropriate in the setting of a public school.

Legal rulings in the twentieth century have jeopardized free religious expression. As a result, public schools have grown increasingly hostile to the rights of students to express religious opinions. This policy analysis is intended to give clarity to the current discussion of prayer in the public schools, in relation to the Free Exercise Clause of the United States Constitution.

The First Amendment

Twentieth-century court decisions have placed the question of school prayer under the rubric of the First Amendment to the U.S. Constitution. The applicable part of that amendment reads:

> Congress shall make no law respecting an establishment of religion [Establishment Clause], or prohibiting the free exercise thereof [Free Exercise Clause];

In order to answer the question of whether or not prayer as religious expression has any place in public education, we must understand three things:

- The contextual history of the Constitution
- The textual history of the First Amendment
- The origin of the phrase "separation of church and state"

This paper addresses each of these and compares the findings to the decisions of applicable U.S. Supreme Court cases.

Historical Context of the Constitution

When the Constitutional Convention first met in Philadelphia in 1787, the religious landscape of the states was varied. Most states gave official recognition to one established religious denomination. The state of Virginia, for example, recognized the Episcopal Church as representative of the state. Religious belief as an integral part of colonial life was not in question. Rather, religious problems that arose among states centered on the differences among states' established denominations.

The political landscape also bore marks of disunity. The Articles of Confederation had proved insufficient for governing, and the states were fighting over issues of taxation—namely, who should pay the costs incurred by the Revolutionary War. As the Constitutional Convention convened, observers said the idea of a Constitu-

"Public schools have grown increasingly hostile to the rights of students to express religious opinions."

tion, much less a nation, was fragile and quickly vanishing. Chaired by George Washington, this meeting of some of the original Founders was seen as a last attempt at unity.

During the Constitutional Convention, states squabbled and self-interest abounded, to the point that no progress was being made. It was then that an aged Ben Franklin stood and said:

> "In the beginning of the contest with Britain, when we were sensible of danger, we had *daily prayers* in this room for Divine protection. *Our prayers*, Sir, were heard, and they were graciously answered. All of us who were engaged in the struggle must have observed frequent instances of a superintending providence in our favor . . . and have we now forgotten this powerful Friend? Or do we imagine we no longer need His assistance?
>
> I have lived, Sir, a long time, and the longer I live, the more convincing proofs I see of this truth: 'that God governs in the affairs of man.' And if a sparrow cannot fall to the ground without His notice, is it probable that an empire can rise without His aid?
>
> I therefore beg leave to move that, *henceforth, prayers imploring the assistance of Heaven and its blessings on our deliberations be held in this assembly every morning before we proceed to business* [emphasis added]."

The 81-year-old Benjamin Franklin was not one of the more religiously-minded Founding Fathers—he actually believed more in the rational views of the French Enlightenment—yet he was willing to acknowledge the importance of prayer to the political aspirations of a nation. Not a prayer bound to a *denomination*, like the states already had, but prayer that acknowledged God as the Creator and Sustainer, prayer that superseded the petty factions of "officially recognized" establishments.

Historical Text of the First Amendment

After the Constitution was written, the first 10 amendments, known as the Bill of Rights, were added to ensure the maintenance of certain liberties not expressly stated in the Constitution. James Madison wrote the First Amendment "religion clauses," and an earlier draft made his intentions clear:

> The civil rights of none shall be abridged on account of religious belief or worship, nor shall any national religion be established.

When the Antifederalists [a political group that opposed a strong federal government] saw the word "national" in Madison's earlier draft, they argued that his use of that word presupposed a powerful centralized government. That was not Madison's intention, so his wording was changed to the present construction. Yet understanding the wording of Madison's first draft shows that he intended to alleviate the fear that a national church, such as the Anglican Church in Great Britain, would rise to official preeminence.

Separation of Church and State

The phrase "separation of church and state" is not mentioned in the U.S. Constitution, because its drafters did not see a dichotomy between their religious beliefs and the document that constructed their Republic. The phrase "separation of church and state" came primarily from two sources, a letter Thomas Jefferson wrote to a group of ministers and from the U.S. Supreme Court case, *Everson v. Board of Education.*

The Danbury Letter. Thomas Jefferson wrote the famous phrase "separation of church and state" in a letter to the Committee of the Danbury Baptist Association in Connecticut. He was responding to the letter they had written, part of which said:

> "Our Sentiments are uniformly on the side of Religious Liberty—That Religion is at all times and places a Matter between God and Individuals—That no man ought to suffer in Name, person or effects on account of his religious Opinions—That the legitimate Power of civil Government extends no further than to punish the man who works ill to his neighbor."

Jefferson's response to their letter was amicable. He said,

> "Believing with you that religion is a matter which lies solely between man and his God, that he owes account to none other for his faith or his worship,

that *the legislative powers of government reach actions only, and not opinions* [emphasis added], I contemplate with sovereign reverence that act of the whole American people which declared that their legislature should 'make no law respecting an establishment of religion, or prohibiting the free exercise thereof,' thus building a wall of separation between Church and State. Adhering to this expression of the supreme will of the nation in behalf of the *rights of conscience*, I shall see with sincere satisfaction the progress of those sentiments which tend to restore to man all his natural rights, convinced he has no natural right in opposition to his social duties."

Jefferson's declaration of "a wall of separation between Church and State" expressed his opinion that the federal government did not have the authority to "prescribe even occasional performances of [religious] devotion." He did not question the validity of religious belief, but he constructed his "wall" to protect religious freedom of conscience from the potential of one federally recognized religion. His fears were well founded. In his Inaugural Address of the previous year, Jefferson had noted that America had "banished from our land that religious intolerance under which mankind so long bled and suffered." Clearly, Jefferson decried the federal domination of religious freedom through one established church.

In addition, when Jefferson founded the University of Virginia, the Pamphlet of University Regulations included two sections that read:
- No compulsory attendance on prayers or services.
- Each denomination to send a clergyman to conduct daily prayers and Sunday service for two weeks.

Was this a man who would have sanctioned the complete removal of any form of prayer from the public schools of America? Obviously, Thomas Jefferson's views on church and state have been grossly distorted.

Everson v. Board of Education. The second notable mention of the phrase "separation of church and state" came in the 1947 U.S. Supreme Court case, *Everson v. Board of Education.* The plaintiff argued the New Jersey law that reimbursed parents for the cost of bus transportation—to public and religious schools—violated the Establishment Clause of the First Amendment. The Supreme Court said that it did not. In the majority opinion, however, Justice Hugo Black used language to set the stage for damaging rulings in the future. He wrote that the Establishment Clause created a "complete separation between the state and religion." Jefferson's letter was written 10 years after the ratification of the First Amendment, yet Black relied upon his own interpretation of Jefferson's words, rather than on the text of the First Amendment, to set the *Everson* precedent for future rulings.

> *"The men who hammered out each section of the Constitution also believed in the importance of daily prayer."*

Chapter 2

Twentieth-Century Cases

Twentieth-century courts, based predominately on Jefferson's letter and on the precedent Justice Black created in *Everson*, have argued that the Constitution intended to separate all religious expression from public life. Yet that ignores the textual history and the original intent of James Madison, the author of these religion clauses. It also ignores the broad, historical context. The men who hammered out each section of the Constitution also believed in the importance of daily prayer.

The Establishment Clause has often been misinterpreted to mean that any link to religion is "establishing" religion. One of the causes of this is a simple alteration of the wording in the First Amendment. The clause reads, "Congress shall make no law respecting *an* establishment of religion." It does *not* read, "Congress shall make no law respecting *the* establishment of religion," as it is often misquoted. If

> *"Schools can allow free religious expression without* embracing *any particular type of religious thought."*

the article is read as "the," then it refers to establishment of all religion in general. If the article is "an," then it clearly refers to a specific religion or denomination—an interpretation backed up by historical records. Realizing that the amendment uses the word "an" helps clarify the meaning of the Framers. So, rather than attempting to separate themselves from religious belief and expression, the Framers were trying to keep one *denomination* from being favored over another.

The twentieth-century cases pertinent to the issue of school prayer do not recognize those differences. They have clearly been built upon the framework created by *Everson*, as summaries of key cases demonstrate:

- *McCollum v. Board of Education* (1948). It is a violation of the Establishment Clause for Jewish, Catholic or Protestant religious leaders to lead optional/voluntary religious instruction in public school buildings.
- *Engel v. Vitale* (1962). The daily recitation of prayer in public schools is unconstitutional.
- *Abington School District v. Schempp* (1963). Daily school-directed reading of the Bible (without comment), and daily recitation of the Lord's Prayer, violates the Establishment Clause when performed in public schools.
- *Lemon v. Kurtzman* (1971). This ruling created the three-part "Lemon test" for determining violations of the Establishment Clause. To avoid a violation, an activity must meet the following criteria: 1) have a secular purpose; 2) not advance or inhibit religion (in principle or primary effect); 3) not foster excessive entanglement between the government and religion.
- *Stone v. Graham* (1980). The Court struck down a state law requiring public schools to post the Ten Commandments (with a notice of "secular application").

- *Wallace v. Jaffree* (1985). A state law requiring a moment of "meditation or voluntary prayer" was struck down as an establishment of religion because the intent of the legislature was deemed to be religious rather than secular.
- *Lee v. Weisman* (1992). A private, nongovernmental individual (in this case a rabbi) at a public school graduation cannot offer prayer. Student rights were infringed upon, according to the Court, because the important nature of the event in effect compelled them to attend graduation. That, in effect, compelled students to bow their heads and be respectful during the prayer, which the Court ruled was a constitutional violation.
- *Santa Fe Independent School District v. Jane Doe* (2000). The Court struck down a school district's policy that allowed an elected student chaplain to open football games with a public prayer. Even though high school football games are purely voluntary activities, the Court concluded that the policy "establishes an improper majoritarian election on religion, and unquestionably has the purpose and creates the perception of encouraging the delivery of prayer at a series of important school events."

Notice that each of those cases focused on the Establishment Clause to the *detriment* of the Free Exercise Clause. That has been the trend of the twentieth century. The courts have too quickly forgotten that the Constitution explicitly protects the free exercise of religion.

Arguments Against School Prayer

While the Founding Fathers encouraged prayer during the Constitutional Convention and in ordinances governing education, the U.S. Supreme Court has dramatically shifted their original premises. Some legal scholars and special interest groups have built upon those precedents, creating other rationalizations for limiting religious expression in America's public schools.

The most prevalent argument of such individuals is that the government has a responsibility to be neutral, so that no child is offended by the religious speech of another. This is erroneous because the issue *cannot* be neutral. Elimination of religious expression for the atheist will offend the child who believes in God. So, the schools must choose. Since 1962, they have sided with the small, nonreligious minority of atheists which, as a recent *Newsweek* poll shows, consists of only 4 percent of the population. By contrast, 94 percent of respondents to that same survey professed a religious faith, and 61 percent said that they agreed with the statement that "religion is very important" in their lives.

If free religious expression in the form of prayer is prohibited, school officials are, at the very least, teaching children that public acknowledgment of God is not as important as the things the schools *can* discuss. It seems unreasonable that public schools allow open discussion about sex but do not allow open discussion about God. The courts have forgotten that schools can allow free religious expression without *embracing* any particular type of religious thought.

Another argument used against religious expression is that prayer "polarizes citizens around a religious axis." Yet the First Amendment was written to *avoid* the squabbles that might result among denominations. Not allowing prayer has done more to polarize citizens than almost any other issue in American history. Allowing prayer would put decision-making back in the hands of parents and local school boards, where it once rested. Those local boards could set guidelines that would allow students who object to all prayer or some prayers not to participate, just as many religious students have opted out of sex education classes. That would clearly respect the rights of the minority, without infringing upon the rights of the majority. Local school boards would also be protected by the constitutional "time/place/manner" restrictions that apply equally to religious and nonreligious speech. Ultimately, a restoration of free expression to local public schools would unite, not polarize, citizens.

Freedom of Religion: An Inalienable Right

The Constitution grants the free exercise of religion to every American, and that right should not vanish at the doors of a public school. Although the Constitution does not overtly mention God, it does imply dependence upon a Creator through its last words, called the Subscription Clause. It says:

> Done in convention, by the unanimous consent of the states present, the Seventeenth day of September, in the Year of our Lord One Thousand Seven Hundred and Eighty-Seven, and of the independence of the United States of America the twelfth. In witness whereof we have hereunto subscribed our names.

The fact that the Founding Fathers recognized the Constitution as written in the *12th* year of independence, shows the Declaration of Independence to be America's founding document. The Declaration clearly acknowledges the Creator God.

The Founders did not codify religion in the Constitution because Congress did not have the authority to govern religious thought. As James Madison so aptly put it, "Religion is the duty man owes to his Creator." The members of Congress did not desire to create a theocratic form of government, because religious belief is not under the jurisdiction of civil government.

Yet just as government does not have the right to impose religion, government also does not have the authority to constrain free religious expression. The Declaration of Independence did not infringe upon the multiplicity of modes of worship in the states, yet it acknowledged God and unchangeable universal principles, as inalienable rights.

That balance is still possible today. Congress must now meet the challenge presented to them. Americans overwhelmingly favor a remedy for the jurisprudence of error that has suppressed their rights of free exercise for too many years. Let us return to our heritage as a free nation, unencumbered by the bonds that have too easily entangled us.

Faith-Based Social Services Organizations Should Be Eligible for Federal Funding

by Leslie Lenkowsky

About the author: *Leslie Lenkowsky is a professor of philanthropic studies and public policy at Indiana University-Purdue University in Indianapolis.*

On the campaign trail [in 2000], George W. Bush staked a large part of his claim to "compassionate conservatism" on the belief that a range of social services now run by secular agencies could be more effectively administered by religious groups—groups that had shown the ability, as he declared on the stump, "to save and change lives." So it was no surprise that one of Bush's first major initiatives as President was to open a new White House office devoted to lending support to "faith-based" organizations whose services include things like family counseling, operating homeless shelters, and the rehabilitation of criminals.

As a practical matter, the plan outlined by the President in January [2001] did indeed hold out the promise of significant new resources for such organizations. It proposed, in the first place, a number of changes in the tax code aimed at spurring private giving, the most notable being a measure to allow far more Americans to deduct charitable contributions from their taxes. More ambitiously, the administration declared its intention to make faith-based organizations full participants in the multibillion-dollar competition for federal social-service grants and contracts. As the White House made clear, the first order of business for John J. DiIulio, Jr., the University of Pennsylvania social scientist appointed to head the Office of Faith-Based and Community Initiatives, would be to conduct a comprehensive review of the laws and regulations that have so far prevented such groups from taking a "seat at the table" alongside their secular counterparts.

For all the fanfare, and controversy, with which these ideas were presented and received by the press, their recent history extends back to well before the Bush campaign. In 1996, a bipartisan coalition in Congress had added to the welfare-reform law a provision called "charitable choice," which allowed religious groups to use government funds for helping welfare recipients. Similar provisions were later included in three other social-service programs, and the Clinton administration even chose a Catholic priest to oversee "community and interfaith partnerships" at the Department of Housing and Urban Development. Nonetheless, the bureaucratic obstacles to the participation of faith-based organizations

> *"A remarkable three out of four Americans support [government funding for faith-based social-service organizations]."*

remained formidable, and few groups felt that their services were in fact welcome—a situation that Bush is plainly determined to reverse.

That determination, entailing as it does a real and far-reaching transformation in how government provides social services, is what has brought down upon the Bush proposals a remarkably broad chorus of criticism. As expected, groups like the American Civil Liberties Union, which have long opposed any sort of public support for religious institutions, have registered their objections. But so too, and quite unexpectedly, have a range of religious organizations and leaders, including many of the Christian conservatives whose support was crucial to Bush's election. None of this has stopped the White House and its allies in Congress from moving forward with legislation to promote faith-based programs—and indeed, according to a recent poll by the Pew Forum on Religion and Public Life, a remarkable three out of four Americans support the idea in principle. But just months after being introduced, the centerpiece of the new administration's domestic policy now faces considerably dimmer prospects.

A Chorus of Criticism

The arguments that have been made against the Bush plan fall under several broad headings. The taxonomy is complicated somewhat by the fact that under certain of these rubrics, attacks have come from both the Left and the Right, though of course for different reasons.

The first objection is that government support for faith-based organizations violates the First Amendment's stricture against the "establishment" of religion, breaching the "wall of separation" (the phrase is Thomas Jefferson's) between church and state. As civil libertarians see it, the Bush administration's proposals would put the government in the untenable position of picking and choosing among religious groups, a sure invitation, in their view, to favoritism as well as to religious strife.

For their part, leaders of the religious Right have expressed precisely the opposite fear: they worry that the government will find itself obliged to support groups whose beliefs and practices are outside the American mainstream. Pat Robertson of the Christian Coalition has said that the Bush plan would open a "Pandora's box," and the Reverend Jerry Falwell has singled out Islam as a faith that should not receive public funds because, he has alleged, it preaches hatred. Nor are they alone in these concerns. Half of those surveyed by Pew are opposed to seeing government funds wind up in the coffers of mosques, Buddhist temples, or the Church of Scientology.

The second broad set of objections has to do with the effect that public support would have on religious charities themselves. As the White House has emphasized—and as existing "charitable choice" laws already mandate—only the nonreligious services provided by a faith-based organization would be eligible for direct government funding, and clients may not be proselytized or required to take part in religious activities.

But according to Marvin Olasky, a journalism professor at the University of Texas whose writings were a primary inspiration for "compassionate conservatism," imposing this sort of divide is neither possible nor desirable. Many faith-based organizations, he recently observed, citing Teen Challenge, a well-known and avowedly Christian program for juvenile drug and alcohol abusers, "cannot separate counseling and evangelism. Evangelism is [their] counseling." In Olasky's view, forcing such groups to refrain from religious activities essentially reduces them to secular charities—and thereby greatly diminishes their prospects for success.

Thirdly, liberal critics have charged that if faith-based organizations receive government support, they will not be held to the standards of accountability that apply to other publicly funded entities. Of special concern in this regard is discrimination in hiring. Religious groups, it is feared, will not only exclude workers who do not share their faith but will make other supposedly invidious distinctions, as happened recently in Kentucky, where (in a much-publicized case) a Baptist-run home for at-risk children fired an employee upon discovering she was a lesbian.

Under this same heading of accountability, yet another concern has been raised: that faith-based organizations are not equipped to handle the fiscal and institutional demands that go along with receiving government money. A study conducted in Indianapolis, where a prototype of

> *"Courts have fairly consistently held that faith-based organizations may receive government aid so long as it is used for legitimate public purposes."*

the Bush administration's program has been in operation for several years, found that religious charities did not compare well in this respect to their secular counterparts: their proposals were poorly written, lacked clear budgets and plans for evaluation, and did not include properly credentialed staff. Such lax practices also appear to be responsible in part for instances in which religious groups have defrauded the government, the most notorious recent case—because the perpetrators were among President Clinton's last-minute pardons—being the involvement of four Hasidic Jews from New York State in a bogus religious school that received federal money for student aid.

A final and potentially decisive objection to expanding "charitable choice" is that faith-based organizations simply do not work. At the very least, there is no empirical evidence demonstrating that they are more effective than existing federal grantees. As Byron R. Johnson, a social scientist at the University of Pennsylvania who has tried to measure the influence of religion on social problems, recently told the *New York Times,* the new White House office promoting the faith-based idea has been constructed "out of anecdotes."

Addressing First Amendment Concerns

None of these varied criticisms is trivial, and few of them can be answered with perfect assurance. Nevertheless, and even taken together, they do not constitute a telling case against the Bush administration's plan for involving religious groups more deeply in the provision of services to our neediest citizens.

The constitutional issues raised by public funding for faith-based groups are in many respects the easiest to deal with. As has often been pointed out, Jefferson's idea of a "wall of separation" between church and state first appeared in a Supreme Court decision that upheld a degree of state support for a religious institution. In the 1947 case of *Everson v. Board of Education*, Justice Hugo Black ruled that the First Amendment did not prevent New Jersey from allowing students at parochial schools to travel on publicly financed buses. Since then, the courts have fairly consistently held that faith-based organizations may receive government aid so long as it is used for legitimate public purposes—like transporting school children or providing them with computer instruction—and does not serve primarily to advance religion.

What the Bush plan aims to do is nothing more than to bring the administration of social services into line with this constitutional principle. After all, since the advent of the Great Society in the 1960's, public officials have increasingly relied on the nonprofit sector to carry out programs for the disadvantaged. It is estimated that the country's private charities now receive more than a third of their income for social services, health care, and education from public sources. With the government already handing out billions of dollars to secular social-service organizations—including the secular affiliates of the major religious denominations—the real transgression against the Constitution's promise of neutrality would seem to consist of barring qualified faith-based groups from receiving such funds.

Whether these groups are in fact "qualified" will depend, the Bush administration has insisted, solely on their capacity to provide needed services. That this standard runs the risk of placing public funds into the hands of cults and religious extremists cannot be denied. But the risk has been greatly exaggerated.

Aside from the non-Judeo-Christian religions that seem to cause anxiety for Pat Robertson, Jerry Falwell, and, alas, many other Americans, the fact is that few truly objectionable groups are likely to accept the restrictions that will apply to publicly funded religious charities. One somehow doubts, for instance, that the Nation of Islam will be prepared to cooperate with federal rules for financial reporting, much less the requirements that it refrain from religious recruitment in its social services and accept clients regardless of their beliefs.

The Effect of Government Regulations on Faith-Based Organizations

A more legitimate concern is that those very requirements, themselves made necessary by the First Amendment, will rob faith-based groups of whatever advantages they possess by virtue of their religious message.

One possible solution to this difficulty is for such groups simply to forgo public support, relying instead on the higher level of charitable giving that the Bush administration hopes to generate with changes in the tax code. Unfortunately, however, these changes are likely to make only a modest difference. The most significant of them, allowing the 70 percent of taxpayers who do not itemize their deductions to get credit for their charitable gifts, would increase annual donations, according to the most optimistic estimates, by $14 billion—no small amount, but only 10 percent more than what Americans already gave to charity last year. (The actual figure is apt to be even smaller, since many people already give without being able to claim a deduction.) Moreover, to judge by current patterns of giving, less than half of this increase would go to religious groups, and only a fraction of that to their social-service activities.

Nor can much help be expected from the nation's foundations and corporations, which—with notable exceptions like the Lilly Endowment and Wal-Mart—have long been reluctant to support faith-based groups. In 1998, only some 2 percent of the billions of dollars given by the nation's 1,000 largest foundations went to religiously affiliated institutions, and much of that was earmarked for hospitals and universities. As for corporate America, six of the country's ten largest businesses, according to a recent survey by the Capital Research Center, "ban or restrict" donations to religious groups; AT&T's contributions, for instance, are exclusively reserved, as its website announces, for organizations that are "nonsectarian and nondenominational." The Bush administration's initiative, by providing new legitimacy to faith-based organizations, may cause a few big givers to reconsider, but it is unlikely to shake the profound wariness toward religious charities that one finds among the heirs, trustees, and professional staffers who now dominate the philanthropic world.

A more promising solution, as Marvin Olasky and others have suggested (and as the White House seems prepared to accept), would be to rely on vouchers to fund those faith-based social services, like Teen Challenge, whose very essence is religious. Such "pervasively sectarian" institutions may receive public aid, the Supreme Court and a number of lower courts have suggested, when secular options are also available and when the decision to participate is a private one, made by individuals. Though this principle remains in dispute—most notably with respect to school choice—vouchers still represent the best option for including those charities that depend most directly on the power of faith. The real question will be whether these groups can avoid the sorts of rules and restrictions that have followed in the wake of federal voucher programs in areas like Medicare, Medicaid, and financial aid for higher education.

Where Olasky and other conservative critics of the Bush plan go wrong is in suggesting that the only faith-based organizations worth supporting are those that make religious activities an integral part of the services they provide. This is not the case. At root, what makes a group faith-based is the religious commitment of those who run it and their devotion—even if through exclusively secular means—to improving the lives of the most troubled and disadvantaged members of their community.

Many such groups are no doubt also interested in winning converts, and should be able to continue doing so independently, with their own resources and on their own time. All that is required is recognizing the difference between saving souls and meeting more mundane needs. That faith-based groups will inevitably fail to respect any such distinction was the burden of a recent article in the *New York Times.* In El Salvador, the paper reported, officials of the U.S. Agency for International Development (AID) felt they had to withdraw the government contract of an evangelical Christian group, Samaritan's Purse, that had come to provide earthquake relief. The reason: its members had conducted prayer sessions before showing Salvadorans how to build new homes.

What the story actually demonstrated, however, was something else entirely: that faith-based groups already make a conscientious effort to obey federal guidelines. AID officials may not have been "comfortable" with the religious activities of Samaritan's Purse, as they told the *Times,* but the money for the prayer sessions had come from the group's own funds, and the participation of the Salvadorans was in no way a condition of their receiving help.

> *"Faith-based organizations— like any other government contractor—must abide by the regulations [regarding discrimination in the workplace]."*

As the Bush administration recognizes—and as religious charities themselves often complain—the rules governing such arrangements could stand some elaboration. No one thinks it will be easy to establish clear boundaries between secular and spiritual activities, but the federal bureaucracy has already had to wrestle with defining these gray areas—it is hardly an insurmountable task.

For their part, faith-based groups are justified to some extent in their worry that government money will come with strings attached—it always does—and may interfere with their separate pursuit of religious ends. Here too, however, the record is largely encouraging. According to a survey of nonprofit organizations done in the mid-1990's by Stephen V. Monsma of Pepperdine University, only 13 percent of the faith-based groups that received public funds felt any pressure to alter their religious practices. Among those most committed to spreading their faith, the figure was somewhat higher, at 22 percent, but the vast majority reported no problems, and relatively few had limited their own religious activities to avoid government interference.

Holding Funding Recipients Accountable

This brings us to the concern that faith-based organizations will flout other government standards, and thus avoid public accountability. Here, too, there is reassurance in how such groups currently operate. Indeed, the problems most often cited to show their tendency to defy public regulation often show just the opposite.

Consider the case of the lesbian fired by the Baptist children's home in Kentucky, a charity that receives three-quarters of its budget from the state. She claims that the home considered her sexual orientation inconsistent with "Christian values"—something clearly impermissible under current law, which allows faith-based organizations to consider the religious beliefs of an employee only when they bear a "bona fide" relationship to job performance. But the home sees things differently. The woman was dismissed, it claims, not for her beliefs but because "homosexual behavior is not in the best interest of anyone, especially sexually abused and confused children and youth."

The courts will decide which side is right in this case, but the very fact that it is being litigated demonstrates that, far from escaping accountability, faith-based organizations—like any other government contractor—must abide by the regulations. The same lesson is to be drawn from the recent case of the Hasidic Jews and their bogus religious school: though public attention focused on their having won a pardon from Bill Clinton, the more important point as far as the faith-based initiative is concerned is that they had been convicted for their crimes.

For most religious charities, especially in the inner cities, the question is not so much whether they are willing to comply with government regulations as whether they are able to do so. Generally, these small organizations lack the resources of better-heeled charities, everything from computerized accounting systems to professional legal services. But these are not likely to be permanent defects, and the administration has already proposed establishing a pool of money, funded both publicly and privately, to help pay for better training and other forms of assistance. One can also expect that more experienced nonprofit groups would share their expertise.

Even so, it should be emphasized that modestly endowed religious organizations are hardly alone in finding it difficult to navigate the rules imposed by public grants and contracts. Even more sophisticated charities complain about this. Among the chief problems, according to a Clinton administration task force, are excessive paperwork, "duplicative and sometimes contradictory" requirements, and long delays in obtaining approval and funding. As the task force concluded, streamlining this process would benefit all charities, religious or otherwise. Of particular importance to faith-based organizations will be the elimination of arbitrary rules that allow, for example, the use of professional therapy but not pastoral counseling.

The Effectiveness of Faith-Based Social Service Organizations

But the real question is whether any of this will ultimately make a difference in confronting the nation's most serious social problems. That there is little research proving the effectiveness of faith-based groups is not news to their more informed advocates. Even John DiIulio, the head of the White House's initiative, has tried to distance himself from the more extravagant claims of enthusiasts. As he wrote shortly before taking office, "we do not really know whether these faith-based programs . . . outperform their secular counterparts, how they compare to one another, or whether, in any case, it is the 'faith' in 'faith-based' that mainly determines any observed difference."

There are some things, however, we do know about faith-based charities, starting with the fact of their near-ubiquity. As the sociologist Mark Chaves discovered in a 1998 survey, 57 percent of religious congregations are engaged in providing social services in some fashion. A more recent investigation, done by the Hartford Seminary, puts the figure even higher, at 85 percent of churches, synagogues, mosques, and other "spiritual communities." Studies of particular cities like Philadelphia have found similarly high rates of congregational involvement in helping the needy.

For another thing, it is clear that, at least in the eyes of those who keep them in business by funding them, many existing faith-based groups have done exemplary work. In March [2001], the Robert Wood Johnson Foundation—another in the handful of major philanthropies that support religious groups—announced a $100-million expansion of a program called "Faith-in-Action," which for almost twenty years has been organizing volunteers from religious congregations to care for the elderly, sick, and disabled. Still another success story is Alcoholics Anonymous, whose faith-based program, predicated on the willingness of participants to call upon the help of a "higher power," receives substantial public support, especially in the nation's prisons.

In a broader vein, a number of studies have shown that belonging to a religious group or praying regularly has a positive impact on health, family stability, and other aspects of personal well-being. Couples who worship together have a better chance of staying married; and young, inner-city black men who attend church are more likely to be employed. Even more suggestive is research done in the 1970's by the late sociologist James Coleman, who found that low-income children, regardless of their religious background, performed considerably better in the tradition-minded environment of Catholic schools than in the local public schools.

There is evidence as well that faith-based programs are particularly attractive to the most troubled recipients of social services. A study of Indiana's "Faith Works" program, which allows welfare recipients to get help from religious charities, found that those opting for such charities over their secular alternatives came from more distressed family situations and had deeper personal crises, including serious health problems and homelessness. What these more disadvantaged people found at faith-based organizations, the study concluded, was a measure of emotional and spiritual support that other charities, focused as they were on material aid, did not provide.

None of this, needless to say, makes an airtight case. When it comes to the better behavior of churchgoers, for example, the key factor may be not so much going to church as being the sort of person who chooses to go to church. (Similar charges were made against Coleman's research on Catholic schools, though he controlled for this possibility in various ways.) Indeed, it is the lack of reliable information on the efficacy of faith-based groups that has led DiIulio and others to insist that evaluation and, to the extent possible, rigorous research play an important role in the President's initiative.

> *"For [faith-based charities], the answers to poverty, crime, and addiction lie . . . in old-fashioned virtues like diligence, self-control, sobriety, and, of course, faith."*

But it is easy to get carried away by the demand for hard social-scientific evidence. Such evidence is notoriously difficult to obtain—complex public programs being anything but controlled experiments—and, more to the point, it has never been demanded of the secular nonprofit groups that for decades have served as the chief agents of the American welfare state. What faith-based organizations bring to the debate, at least at this early point, is not a track record of proven achievement but a great deal of promise—and an old, if now seemingly revolutionary, idea about the roots of genuine social change.

Bringing Morality Back to Government Charity

In the end, what is distinctive about the President's plan is not its reliance on proxies to provide the federal government's social services—this, as not a few worried conservatives have observed, was a key innovation of the Great Society. What is distinctive, rather, is its unabashedly moral tone. That tone is a throwback to an era when the nation's charities were concerned not just about the material circumstances of those they helped but about their character and behavior as well.

Liberals may dismiss such notions as nostalgia for a tradition of American philanthropy that gave us poorhouses and orphanages; but liberals, who have their own sins to live down when it comes to the policies they have sponsored, are not in the best position to mock. Above all, as Myron Magnet writes in introducing a recent collection of essays from *City Journal*, that older tradition emphasized "the attitudes of self-reliance and personal responsibility," and the need to spark "an inner change in the recipient." Nor, in taking this approach to the immigrant underclass of a century ago, were reformers indifferent to wider social and economic conditions. But, as Joel Schwartz observes in his illuminating study, *Fighting Poverty with Virtue*, they did evaluate any proposed public policy in terms of its tendency to reinforce behavior that would allow the needy to succeed on their own, a task at which the liberal social policies of the last decades notoriously failed.

The most visible modern descendants of this older tradition of charity are faith-based organizations, especially those that operate through the black churches of the country's big cities. For them, the answers to poverty, crime, and addiction lie not in the ministrations of social workers and government bureaucrats but in old-fashioned virtues like diligence, self-control, sobriety, and, of course, faith. It is these groups that are most eager to win government support for their efforts: in a recent survey, some two-thirds of black congregations signaled an interest in public dollars, as compared to just over a quarter of predominantly white churches.

For these financially strained organizations, already deeply involved in our inner cities, a far-reaching expansion of "charitable choice" would be a figurative if not a literal godsend, allowing them to influence their communities as never before. Conservatives will continue to fret about the specter of heavy-handed regulation, and liberals about public funds going to groups that speak freely of vice, sin, and salvation. But when the dust settles, we may have moved a step closer to restoring religious groups to their rightful place in the public square— and significant numbers of truly disadvantaged Americans might at last receive assistance more useful than yet another handout.

[Editor's note: As of June 2002, Congress has yet to approve President Bush's initiative to offer faith-based charities federal money.]

The Constitution's Framers Intended Strict Separation of Church and State

by Allen Jayne

About the author: *Allen Jayne is the author of* Jefferson's Declaration of Independence: Origins, Philosophy, and Theology.

Separation of church and state, a cornerstone of American civilization, has been under attack for several years. The Reverend Pat Robertson, for example, has long maintained such separation does not exist. Few people, outside of the Christian right, have taken him seriously. In the summer of 1998, however, a new attack was made—this time on the ideas of Thomas Jefferson, a principal architect of separation of church and state.

In his interpretation of a recent FBI study, James Hutson, chief of manuscripts at the Library of Congress, makes three conclusions about Jefferson. First, Jefferson's famous "wall of separation between Church and State" letter to the Baptists of Danbury, written in 1802, was based solely on politics, not philosophy. Second, he came to believe that traditional religion was important in the sense of essential to the morals of a republic. Third, he was not serious about separating church and state.

All of Hutson's conclusions are erroneous.

Jefferson's Philosophical Beliefs

In the first, although Hutson correctly states Jefferson's letter served a political purpose, simultaneously it states a philosophical principle that was a basis of John Locke's concept of toleration put to use in American law by Jefferson and James Madison. Prior to and during Locke's time, it was difficult to determine where religion or church left off and government or state began. The powers of both were often combined. As a result, churches frequently used the force of the state to promote and enforce their interests and doctrines. This caused horrendous atrocities against Jews and heretics, as well as the European religious wars between Catholics and Protestants of the sixteenth and seventeenth centuries that resulted in the deaths of millions of people.

In order to prevent such bloodshed, Locke attacked the combination of church and state that caused it in his Letter Concerning Toleration. Jefferson read this work carefully. In it is found the philosophical basis of Jefferson's "wall of separation" comment made as respects the First Amendment's language: "Congress shall make no law respecting an establishment of religion or prohibiting the free exercise thereof."

Locke argued in his Letter that church and state had separate interests and functions. The church's interest was "the salvation of souls" and therefore sacred. Its function was to provide a system of beliefs and a form of worship conducive to salvation.

The interest of the state, on the other hand, was secular, having to do with "life, liberty, health . . . and the possession of outward things, such as money, lands, houses, furniture, and the like." The state's, or state magistrate's, function was "to secure unto all the people in general, and to every one of his subjects in particular, the just possession of these things belonging to this life."

Locke believed force was necessary to perform the state's function that included "the punishment of those that violated any other man's rights." Force, however, was alien to salvation—the church's interest and function. Locke maintained that "true religion consists in the inward and full persuasion of the mind" as respects profession of beliefs and what we are "fully satisfied in our mind . . . is well pleasing unto God" as respects worship. If force was used to compel humans to profess what they did not believe in their minds and to worship in a form they deemed unacceptable to God, they were adding to their "other sins those also of hypocrisy," which prevents salvation.

In the Virginia Statute for Religious Freedom, written by Jefferson in 1777, Locke's idea that the functions of church and state were separate, and that the use of force in religion or church was no part of either of those functions, was made law. Significantly, James Madison was instrumental in the passage of that statute and well aware of its Lockean separation of church and state philosophical foundation.

Just as significantly, it was Jefferson who persuaded Madison to add the Bill of Rights to the Constitution, which included the right of religious freedom, finally made law in 1791. In the First Amendment's religious freedom provisions, Madison used

> *"[Thomas Jefferson] was firmly committed to the rule of human-made law and opposed to that of scripture or God's revealed law in government."*

language that keeps the force of governmental law out of religion and religion supported by the laws of the state out of the state.

It was in this philosophical context, not just the immediate political situation of 1802, that Jefferson praised the First Amendment for building a "wall of separation between Church and State."

Jefferson made two other separations related to church and state: governmental law from church or religious sources and public education from church influence. He was firmly committed to the rule of human-made law and opposed to that of scripture or God's revealed law in government. He got this idea from Lord Bolingbroke's writings. Rule by God's law meant theocracy, whereas human-made law meant democracy—and Jefferson was a thoroughgoing advocate of democracy in the form of a republic.

As for public education, one of its principal purposes, according to Jefferson, was to develop the independent reason of children so that when they matured they could make independent rational judgments on what was best for the state. He wished to keep such education free from the clergy's influence, which, he maintained, brainwashed students and thereby produced citizens dependent on church, scripture, or clergy for knowledge of what was best for the state. This in effect resulted in an oligarchy of the clergy, since they controlled the churches and scriptural interpretations that, in turn, gave them control of the doctrinal and moral thinking of their congregations—a control or authority that often extended to political decisions. This control defeated the democratic principle that each individual should make his or her own decisions in political matters.

> *"There are . . . those in America who would destroy Jefferson and Madison's Lockean wall [between church and state] by chipping away at it little by little."*

Hutson's second conclusion—that Jefferson came to believe that traditional religion was important in the sense of essential to the morals of a republic—is also erroneous because of Jefferson's commitment to Lockean ideas, except that this time those ideas came from the Second Treatise on Government. The Second Treatise, a source of the political philosophy Jefferson placed in the Declaration of Independence, in effect denied the fallen person concept of human nature.

The fallen person was tainted or morally defective and therefore could not be relied upon to obtain uncorrupt moral knowledge independent of God, scripture, church, or clergy. This was the premise of medieval politics, which maintained that only the church and kings anointed or deputized by God via the church were deemed capable of determining the moral direction of the state, since the fall left the people morally incompetent for this task.

In the Second Treatise, Locke turned these elements of medieval politics upside down. There he said in effect that people are not morally incompetent. They can find right and wrong on their own, independent of any church, scripture, clergy, king anointed by God, or noble. Therefore, the people are and should be the final judge of the moral direction of the state and its rulers.

Easy individual access to uncorrupt moral knowledge independent of religion and the ruler of the state is the cornerstone of Lockean political philosophy put forth in the Second Treatise to which Jefferson subscribed all his life. Jefferson, however, rejected Locke's views and adopted those of the Scottish thinker Lord Kames on how individuals easily attained moral knowledge that made traditional religion superfluous as a source of moral knowledge in a republic.

> *"The wall [between church and state] protects . . . religious minorities from being repressed."*

In his third error, Hutson concludes that Jefferson's attending weekly worship services in the House of Representatives, beginning just a few days after his "wall" letter, plus his allowing worship in federal buildings, means he was not serious about church and state separation. However, Jefferson, then president, had powers equal but not superior to those of the House. As a result, he could not terminate worship in the legislative chamber approved by the legislative body. He could only condone such worship, which he no doubt attended because of his strong, although unorthodox, religious instinct. Jefferson loved worship and attended services all his life, mostly at churches whose doctrines he rejected.

The Importance of Separation Between Church and State

There are, of course, those in America who would destroy Jefferson and Madison's Lockean wall by chipping away at it little by little. They would bring God and religion into the state and its institutions, including its schools. But if there were no wall, whose God or religion would it be? Catholic or Protestant, Jewish or Muslim, Hindu or Buddhist? And who would decide this question? The majority? The courts? And would the minority religions that lost out go down without a fight? Or if they did not fight, would they support their government in times of crisis?

History teaches us that men and women have fought and died when their religion was repressed or overwhelmed by their government—or if they did not fight, they did not support their government in times of crises. Locke knew this and wrote about it. So did Jefferson and Madison, and this is why they implemented Locke's ideal of separating church and state with the laws of our land— an ideal that was Locke's plan to preserve religious peace and foster broad support of government within a state.

This plan has worked in the United States. Jefferson stated in 1808 that it brought us "quiet" and "comfort" or religious peace. Since its inception, the United States has never had a religious war despite divisive sectarian differences. And in times of crisis, minority religions have supported the government because it has, for the most part, maintained a position of neutrality among its many religions and denominations. This is because the "wall" or religious freedom law causes all religious groups to be seen and treated equally in the eyes of that law—or, as Jefferson put it, has the effect of "putting all on equal footing."

It is precisely this egalitarian aspect of American law, however, that rankles some of our most prominent religious groups, since they believe they are superior to all others. Indeed, virtually all religions and denominations in the United States have the feeling and consciousness of superiority. Yet only some of the prominent ones, which think they have or can get enough political power to force the government to give them some form of legalized special privilege they believe they deserve because of their claimed superiority, seek such privilege.

Any law, however, that has the effect of providing special privilege or advantage to any religion or denomination causes the beneficiaries to fall within the broad definition of an established or government-sponsored religion outlawed by the First Amendment's language, "Congress shall make no law respecting an establishment of religion." Such law, whether passed through legislation or the result of Supreme Court rulings, would knock down that wall of separation.

And once down, there would surely be a struggle among the major sectarian denominations to win the greatest support of government and its laws and thereby become dominant. Historically such competition has almost always produced violent conflict, not to mention resentment against government by minority religions bound to lose out in such struggles for religious preeminence within a state.

The wall, therefore, protects the United States from religious strife among competing majority religions and denominations, as well as religious minorities from being repressed by those majorities. Religious strife and repression, with all their bloody consequences, have been present in the West where there was no wall and are still present throughout the world where it does not exist.

Isn't it time, therefore, we stop trying to breach or knock down our philosophical-legal wall of separation, or to claim that it does not exist—either outright, as does Pat Robertson, or by inference, as does James H. Hutson? And isn't it time we say, "Thank you, John Locke, Thomas Jefferson, and James Madison" for our wall and the religious peace and tolerance it has brought to our land?

School Prayer Threatens Religious Liberty

by Americans United for Separation of Church and State

About the author: Americans United for Separation of Church and State is a nonprofit advocacy organization.

As church-state separation battles have escalated in recent decades, so too have misconceptions about the role of religion in public schools. Some Religious Right activists charge that the courts have misinterpreted the First Amendment to remove all traces of religion from the classroom. Has God been expelled from our schools? Has the Bible been excluded from school curriculum?

In reality, the answer to these questions is "no." In order to begin to clear up some of the misunderstanding about religion's place in our schools, it is important for Americans to have the facts.

The debate regarding religion in our classrooms is by no means a recent phenomenon. With the development of the American public school system in the 19th century, controversy erupted about the place of religious values and convictions in schools that welcomed children of many faiths (and none). In some communities, these questions led to bitter conflict and debate. In Philadelphia, for example, full-scale riots and bloodshed erupted in the 1840s over which version of the Bible should be used in classroom devotions. In Cincinnati, a "Bible War" divided the city in the 1870s after the school board discontinued Bible instruction.

Following confrontations like these, many Americans came to realize that interfaith harmony and community goodwill could best be realized by keeping public schools neutral on questions of religion. Contrary to current public perception, state-mandated prayer and Bible reading was not universally practiced in the 19th and early 20th centuries. By the 1950s, fewer than a third of the nation's public school districts had formal religious exercises.

The U.S. Supreme Court affirmed the wisdom of this approach in the early 1960s when it ruled that government-mandated prayer, Bible-reading and other religious devotions are inappropriate in public schools. The justices said the church-state separation provisions of the First Amendment forbade government from interfering with religious matters. Still, even today, some people misunderstand the scope of those decisions.

Although the high court ruled that state-sanctioned prayer in schools is unconstitutional, it did not seek to remove all study about religion. In fact, in *Abington Township School District v. Schempp* (1963), the justices maintained that a student's education is not complete without instruction on the influence of religion on history, culture and literature.

Justice Tom Clark, representing the court, wrote: "Nothing that we have

"Interfaith harmony and community goodwill [can] best be realized by keeping public schools neutral on questions of religion."

said here indicates that such study of the Bible or of religion, when presented objectively as part of a secular program of education, may not be effected consistent with the First Amendment." Clark added that government could not force the exclusion of religion in schools "in the sense of affirmatively opposing or showing hostility to religion."

The court's ruling suggested simply that a student's family, not government, is responsible for decisions about religious instruction and guidance. There was respect, not hostility, toward religion in the court's ruling.

Justice Clark concluded: "The place of religion in our society is an exalted one, achieved through a long tradition of reliance on the home, the church, and the inviolable citadel of the individual heart and mind. We have come to recognize through bitter experience that it is not within the power of government to invade that citadel, whether its purpose or effect be to aid or oppose, to advance or retard. In the relationship between man and religion, the State is firmly committed to a position of neutrality."

Religious Expression Is Allowed in Public Schools

But how is this applicable to public schools? In 1995, a joint statement of current law regarding religion in public schools was published by a variety of religious and civil liberties organizations. This statement served as the basis for U.S. Department of Education guidelines intended to alleviate concerns about constitutional religious activities in schools.

Here are some general rules concerning what school personnel and students may do:

1. Students have the right to pray or to discuss their religious views with their peers so long as they are not disruptive.

2. The history of religion and comparative religion are permissible school subjects so long as the approach is objective and serves a legitimate education purpose.

3. Students may study the role of religion in the history of the United States, and use historic documents such as the Declaration of Independence that contain references to God, provided such documents are not used to promote a religious viewpoint.

4. Schools may discuss various religious groups' beliefs about the origin of life on Earth in comparative religion or social studies classes.

5. Students may express their religious beliefs in the forms of reports, homework and artwork so long as such expression meets the other criteria of the assignment.

6. Religious or anti-religious remarks made in the ordinary course of classroom discussion or student presentations and that are germane are permissible under most circumstances, but students do not have the right to give sermons to a captive audience.

7. Students have the right to distribute religious literature to their classmates, subject to reasonable time, place and manner restrictions.

8. Students have the right to speak to, and attempt to persuade, their peers about religious topics just as they do with regard to political topics. However, students should be aware that repeated attempts to pressure other students to attend religious services or engage in religious activity can be construed as harassment.

9. Student religious clubs in secondary schools must be permitted to meet and to have equal access to campus media to announce their meetings, if a school receives federal funds and permits other student non-curricular clubs to meet during non-instructional time.

10. Public schools may teach objectively about religious holidays and may celebrate the secular aspects of the holiday. Schools may release students to observe religious holidays and functions.

11. Students may wear religious messages on clothing, just as they may wear religious attire, such as yarmulkes and head scarves.

12. Students may be released for religious instruction off school premises.

13. Students may read the Bible or other religious literature during their free time at school.

14. Character traits such as honesty, sportsmanship, courage and civility may be taught, but not as religious tenets.

Schools, however, may not do the following:

1. Teachers and school administrators are prohibited from encouraging or soliciting student religious or anti-religious activity.

2. Schools may not teach creationism, "creation science" or other religiously based concepts in science classes.

3. Schools may not refuse to teach evolutionary theory in order to avoid giving offense to religion.

4. Students may not use a class assignment that calls for an oral presentation as an opportunity to conduct a religious service.

5. Religious leaders or groups may not be given access to classrooms to distribute religious or anti-religious literature.

6. Teachers may not actively participate in sectarian student club activities and "non-school persons" may not direct club meetings (although occasional religious guest speakers are allowed).

7. Schools may not observe religious holidays as religious events.

8. Schools may not allow religious instruction by outsiders on premises during the school day.

"Americans who cherish their freedoms should take alarm at efforts to . . . convert our public schools into Sunday schools."

9. Schools may not provide for compulsory reading from the Bible or other religious literature as part of a devotional activity or religious service.

10. Academic credit may not be given for off-campus religious instruction.

11. Schools may not erect permanent religious symbols in classrooms or post religious scriptures on classroom walls in a way that suggests advocacy of a particular religion.

As is evidenced by these guidelines, the law can be quite clear in providing guidance regarding religion in public schools. In some areas, however, ambiguity remains. State and federal courts are still formulating guidelines on religion's place in public schools. Cases regularly come before the bench for resolution. Keeping informed is the best way for parents and school personnel to guard against actions that may be inconsistent with existing law. Above all, school administrators should proceed with prudence and sensitivity, respecting the beliefs of all students.

Most Americans perceive the rules governing religion and public schools as being fair and helpful in preserving the freedom of conscience of students, parents, and school personnel. Yet there is still a movement under way to destroy the delicate balance we have achieved.

Attacks on Religious Freedom

Unfortunately, some short-sighted politicians and Religious Right activists continue to fight for dangerous constitutional amendments or other measures allowing the government to make decisions about the worship practices of school children. If these efforts are successful, religious majorities in states and localities would be given free rein to impose their religious beliefs on everyone.

America is a diverse nation with over 2,000 identified faith groups. Our public school system must try to serve all students, regardless of background or faith, in an effort to build a common nation. Wrangling over religion is sure to be divisive.

An extraordinary vigilance must be maintained in the face of a relentless assault by misguided sectarian forces. Americans who cherish their freedoms should take alarm at efforts to tear down the wall of separation between church and state and convert our public schools into Sunday schools.

Indeed, most religious denominations, ranging across the theological spectrum, have issued formal statements supporting the Supreme Court's prayer and Bible-reading decisions. These people of faith value the hard-won freedom of conscience that belongs to all of us.

The evidence suggests that advocates of school prayer amendments and similar measures are making every effort to replace our free, non-sectarian public education system with taxpayer-subsidized, church-run academies where only their version of "the truth" is disseminated. In the process, our constitutional traditions would be discarded, and the religious liberties that have allowed all faiths to flourish in America are set aside in some fallacious attempt to help a specific religious agenda. This objective is not only wrong, it's dangerous. It must be stopped.

As Supreme Court Justice Anthony Kennedy, an appointee of President Ronald Reagan, said in a June, 1992 opinion, "No holding of this Court suggests that a school can persuade or compel a student to participate in a religious exercise. . . . The First Amendment's Religion Clauses mean that religious beliefs and religious expressions are too precious to be either proscribed or prescribed by the State."

Faith-Based Social Services Organizations Should Not Be Eligible for Federal Funding

by Gwendolyn Mink

About the author: *Gwendolyn Mink is a professor of politics at the University of California at Santa Cruz.*

Recalling a voluntarism reminiscent of Herbert Hoover, the first President Bush challenged Americans to shine "a thousand points of light" on the nation's social problems. Bush's "thousand points of light" marked a divide between public and private, church and state, for they substituted the power of individual good works for government action. The second President Bush, in contrast, erases the divide, as he espouses government sponsorship of faith-based solutions to social ills and government incentives to teach individuals "the power of faith."

Recalling his father's "thousand points of light," the younger Bush has summoned "armies of compassion" to fulfill government's social policy obligations. But in a bold new departure, he has called upon government to serve the armies of compassion by paying for them to purvey their moral values. Unlike the "thousand points of light," which shined upon a void left by an inactive government, the second Bush's "armies of compassion" have enlisted government in an activist faith-based mission and in turn have been deputized by government to carry that mission out.

Part of this mission is to spread the gospel of faith to single mothers, unwed fathers, substance abusers, the homeless, and the imprisoned. A companion mission is to delegate the delivery of social services from government agencies to proponents of faith. Announcing this two-birds-in-the-bush plan to strengthen governmental moralism and reduce government activity, President Bush has said: "When we see social needs in America, my administration will look first to faith-based programs and community groups, which have proven their power to save and change lives."

The Charitable Choice Concept

The idea that religious organizations are better equipped than government to promote the social welfare was George W. Bush's signature issue during the 2000 presidential campaign. As governor of Texas, he had seized upon a 1996 statutory innovation called "charitable choice" that invited states to delegate welfare programs to religious groups. He applied the charitable choice concept to state-funded programs, as well, such as the InterChange program that offered faith-based counseling to prison inmates and church-run anti-drug programs. During the presidential campaign, he called for federal funding for the Texas prison program and promised to revise laws to allow religious groups "to provide services in every federal, state, and local social program." According to Bush advisor and former Christian Coalition director Ralph Reed, the charitable choice concept was the key to Bush's "compassionate conservatism," for it enabled him to take "the underlying message of traditional values and allowed it to be presented in a nontraditional way that is caring and not judgmental." According to another Bush advisor, *Compassionate Conservatism* author Marvin Olasky, by expanding social ministries charitable choice could also "decrease the need for government action."

Hardly noticed when first enacted, charitable choice was then-Senator John Ashcroft's principal contribution to the 1996 welfare reform law. Charitable choice requires states to permit religious groups to compete to administer welfare programs, including welfare-to-work programs and job training. Texas was one of only four states (the others being Wisconsin, Indiana, and Ohio) to aggressively implement the welfare law's charitable choice rule and one of only a handful of states to do so at all. Although many states remain wary of the constitutional problems posed by charitable choice, President Bush is eager to expand the rule to include drug treatment programs, homeless programs, senior programs, housing, juvenile services, after-school programs, and sexual abstinence education. He also aims to deploy Americorps volunteers as an adjunct army, using federally trained manpower to boost faith-based work.

Federal support for the work of religious organizations is not new: Catholic Charities and Lutheran Social Services, for example, have long relied on federal assistance to operate homeless shelters and soup kitchens. Before 1996, however, religious groups had to set up separate, secular agencies to receive federal money. What is new about charitable choice is that it gives religious groups the right to maintain and express their religious identities, symbols, and philosophies in programs supported by federal dollars. Under charitable choice, federally funded religious groups may not proselytize, but they need not be religion-free. They may not compel church membership or religious conversion among program recipients, but they may hold voluntary prayers, impart religious principles in counseling and other services, and refuse to hire individuals of a different or no faith.

In the years since enactment of the 1996 welfare law, the charitable choice concept has found its way into several other pieces of legislation usually aimed toward poor people. As senator, John Ashcroft (R-Mo.) sponsored legislation to apply charitable choice to every major arena of social services, to extend eligibility to groups that proselytize, and to exempt federally funded faith programs from Title VII's ban on discrimination in employment. Drafters of New Markets, Even Start, substance abuse, and fatherhood promotion bills also adopted charitable choice language. Some of this legislation has stalled, however, in part because of concerns to maintain the church-state divide.

> *"Charitable choice ... brings government directly into the business of establishing religion."*

Making good on his campaign promise to promote religious alternatives to government, President Bush launched his "faith-based initiative" on January 29, 2001. The initiative includes establishment of the White House Office of Faith-Based and Community Initiatives, centers in five cabinet departments to facilitate church-state cooperation, tax cuts for charitable donations, and grants to religious groups. Headed by conservative political scientist and born-again Catholic John DiIulio, the new White House office will review and propose revisions to government regulations that impede participation in government programs by groups with a religious character and mission. It also will lead the effort to proliferate charitable choice provisions in social welfare policy.

The Government Should Not Fund Religious Groups

Bush's promotion of publicly funded, faith-based social welfare programs excites controversy on a number of fronts. First and most obvious, charitable choice crosses the church-state divide by publicly financing institutions that convey religious messages. This brings government directly into the business of establishing religion. While civil libertarians worry about the theocratic implications of government-sponsored religion, some of Bush's partners in "compassionate conservatism," including Marvin Olasky, wonder whether government grants for faith activities might "sap the vitality of religious social programs in the same way that . . . welfare undermined individual initiative among the poor."

A second concern is that charitable choice invites government to express dangerous preferences among religions, as government must decide which faith-based programs to fund. These concerns have been aired widely by Jewish leaders and civil libertarians, as well as by leaders of some mainline Christian denominations. More indicative of the intensity of concern is Pat Robertson's recent warning that "this thing could be a real Pandora's box." In remarks on his "700 Club" television program, the Christian Coalition head and Bush ally worried that the faith-based initiative would benefit non-Christian religious organizations, such as the Church of Scientology and the Unification Church.

A third criticism is that charitable choice requires government to acquiesce to the very employment discrimination it prohibits under the Civil Rights Act, because groups with a religious mission are exempted from major Title VII prohibitions. Another is that charitable choice reorients social policy away from ensuring opportunity and security and toward assuring faith and moral rescue. A fifth objection is that charitable choice moves us down the road toward a government of heavy-handed faith-based rules implemented through privatized, faith-based social service delivery.

Pending lawsuits illuminate the problems posed for religious freedom and employment equality by charitable choice policy. Texas, for example, is being sued by the American Jewish Congress and the Texas Civil Rights Project because the state gave $8,000 to a faith-based jobs program that required participants to study the Bible and biblical values and that taught them "to find employment through a relationship with Jesus Christ." A third of the program's participants reported that they had been pressured to join a church or change their beliefs.

> *"Religious advocacy unfettered by constitutional principles and moral cures for social problems [form] the soul of Bush's faith-based initiative."*

In Wisconsin, meanwhile, the Freedom from Religion Foundation has brought suit against Faith Works, a Milwaukee program to help troubled fathers overcome drug addiction and find jobs, because its bylaws describe it as "inherently Christian" and say it promotes "a holistic, faith-based approach to bring healing to mind, body, heart, and soul." The suit contends that public funding for this program conveys a preference for Christianity.

Finally, in Kentucky, two civil liberties groups have filed suit against the Kentucky Baptist Home for Children because it uses public money to promote a religious agenda and to practice religious discrimination. The home fired a counselor because she is lesbian. A Baptist official said that homosexuality defies the Christian beliefs central to the agency's mission and that the home has a right to fire someone if it does not consider her to be an appropriate role model.

Despite these examples of patent rights violations, President Bush is sticking to his view that a religious group's message is fundamental to the delivery of services. According to Indianapolis Mayor Stephen Goldsmith, advisor to the president on the faith-based initiative and new appointee to the Corporation for National Service (Americorps), "a very important secondary goal is transforming lives through a belief in God and value systems." This combination of interests—religious advocacy unfettered by constitutional principles and moral cures for social problems—forms the soul of Bush's faith-based initiative.

Actually, the faith-based initiative requires relaxed constitutional guarantees.

Otherwise, many of the faith groups upon whose support Bush depends will not take the federal bait. According to a 1998 study, only 28% of conservative, evangelical church leaders said they were willing to take government funding. The evangelical director of Cleveland's City Mission explained: "Even with this talk of faith-based organizations and charitable choice, we've found that there are always strings attached."

The tension between constitutional "strings" and faith-based good works played out in a recent congressional debate about promoting fatherhood. The Child Support Distribution Act of 2000, considered by the House of Representatives in September 2000, included a measure to promote fatherhood by funding programs to provide poor, non-custodial fathers with job training, marriage classes, marriage counseling, relationship instruction, and incentives to live with non-marital children. Seventy-five percent of fatherhood grants were reserved for nongovernmental agencies, including faith-based groups. Representative Bobby Scott (D-Va.) introduced an amendment to forbid faith-based fatherhood program grantees from discriminating against participants and to bar grantees from subjecting participants to sectarian worship and instruction.

The amendment failed after Republican opponents explained that churches would shy away from federal funds if they had to meet nondiscrimination and nonsectarian requirements. These sorts of stipulations would derange the church-state divide, opponents maintained, giving the federal government excuses to meddle in faith-based affairs. Nancy Johnson (R-Conn.), the bill's sponsor, argued that the Scott amendment "would absolutely, without question, chill the participation of the ecumenical community . . . [which] would be a tragedy for men, for families, and for children."

The fatherhood legislation contained in the Child Support Distribution Act of 2000 has not yet become law. Its enactment may be imminent, however, judging from the bipartisan support it enjoys. I have written elsewhere about this legislation's oppressive patriarchalism. Notable here are the ways in which the legislation enlists faith groups, among whose religious tenets is marriage, to teach and counsel poor men to fulfill the secular policy goal of marrying the poor mothers of their biological children. The secular patriarchal goal of restoring the two-parent family, so central to the welfare law of 1996, is fast transposing into the sectarian patriarchal goal of reviving the Christian family.

> *"President Bush's faith-based initiative marks the apogee of government-sponsored religious moralism."*

Less Government, More Religion?

President Bush's faith-based initiative marks the apogee of government-sponsored religious moralism. At the same time, it signals government's retreat from the responsibilities of governing. While the most obvious significance of charitable choice is government's endorsement of religion per se, as well as of such specific religions as receive federal monies, an equally ominous significance is government's delegation of power to the private sector. In fact, charitable choice represents a fusion of the neoliberal urge to privatize and the hard Right's urge to moralize. Brother Jeb Bush has pursued perhaps the clearest path to moralistic privatization in Florida, where the Department of Children and Families has been gradually shifting its responsibilities to faith-based groups with an expectation of totally privatizing child welfare programs in the state by 2003.

Welcoming the second Bush presidency, the Heritage Foundation issued a hefty handbook of Priorities for the President in January 2001. One of its major points is that the 1996 welfare law established a model for future federal-state relations. Although the welfare law ostensibly was a victory for partisans of state flexibility and devolution, Heritage correctly observes that it actually articulated strong national goals and principles to which the states are held accountable. For example, the welfare law declares the national principle that a non-marital mother must make public the identity of her child's biological father, then compels states to enforce the principle by sanctioning mothers who refuse or resist. Bush's faith-based initiative applies this federal-state model of less national governmental activity with more national governmental coercion to the new church-state collaboration. This formula for ruling without responsibility must be why conservatives hunger for national power.

Chapter 3

Is the Right to Privacy Threatened?

Chapter Preface

The right to privacy is not mentioned explicitly anywhere in the Constitution. However, a right to privacy is thought to be inherent in the Fourth Amendment's limits on search and seizure and the Fifth Amendment's protection against self-incrimination. Moreover, as researcher for USConstitution.net Steve Mount explains, "Supreme Court decisions over the years have established that the right to privacy is a basic human right, and as such is protected by virtue of the Ninth Amendment," which states that individuals have rights other than those enumerated in the Constitution.

Many critics fear that the right to privacy—perhaps because it is not explicitly protected by the Constitution—is rapidly eroding as advances in information technology make it easier for governments, corporations, and individuals to pry into people's personal information. Books such as *Database Nation: The Death of Privacy in the 21st Century* and *The End of Privacy: How Total Surveillance Is Becoming a Reality* detail how individuals' personal financial and medical information is available to those willing to purchase or steal it. "As we move into the computerized world of the twenty-first century, privacy will be one of our most important civil rights," writes Simson Garfinkel, author of *Database Nation*. "Technology is killing one of our most cherished freedoms," he maintains. "The shape of our future will be determined in large part by how we understand, and ultimately how we control or regulate, the threats to this freedom that we face today."

Most people agree that an individual should be able to control who has access to his or her personal information. But critics who feel that privacy threats are exaggerated point out that many people willingly sign agreements that allow banks, credit card companies, and retailers to share their customers' financial information with other businesses. "The selling of consumer information has been going on for years and has helped to offset product prices and modernize the country's consumer-related retailers and industries," writes *National Journal* reporter Maureen Sirhal. "Is this good enough reason for Uncle Sam to construct a new system of laws and regulations to protect online privacy?" Some critics suggest that the privacy issue has been blown far out of proportion: "There's a new hysteria over this question of privacy," said Federal Trade Commissioner Thomas Leary in 2001.

As more people conduct financial transactions on the Internet, and as more information is stored in government and corporate databases, the debate over privacy is sure to gain more attention. The viewpoints in the following chapter examine the importance of the right to privacy, and whether this right is in danger.

Loss of Privacy Is a Serious Problem

by Charles J. Sykes

About the author: *Charles J. Sykes is a journalist and the author of* The End of Privacy, *from which the following viewpoint is excerpted.*

"In a few hours, sitting at my computer," writes Carole A. Lane, "beginning with no more than your name and address, I can find what you do for a living, the names and ages of your spouse and children, what kind of car you drive, the value of your house, and how much you pay in taxes on it. From what I learn about your job, your house, and the demographics of your neighborhood, I can make a good guess at your income. I can uncover that forgotten drug bust in college. . . ." If anything, Ms. Lane is being modest.

For a small fee, she can uncover far more about you: your Social Security number, your bank balance, any stock, bonds, and mutual funds you own, your telephone records, your credit history, even your medical history.

Trapped in the Dataweb

For two months in 1997 the Social Security Administration put the detailed income history of millions of Americans on the Internet, where it could easily be accessed with a few pieces of information and keystrokes. It backed off only after a public outcry over potential invasions of privacy. But there are no legal restrictions on the distribution of Social Security numbers by private companies or individuals. Such information is still readily available from a number of private sources.

Even strict rules protecting "confidentiality" of information in government files do not prevent leaks and abuses. A federal audit found that hundreds of IRS employees continue to snoop illegally through confidential taxpayer files. The computerized medical records of tens of millions of patients are especially vulnerable to abuse because there are few controls on the highly confidential medical information that is being widely shared among providers, government agencies, employers, and marketers. In Maryland, state workers sold the names and Social Security numbers of Medicaid recipients to HMO recruiters. Other states keep detailed data banks identifying every patient who stays in a hospital, is injured on the job, gets a flu shot, has a sexually transmitted disease, has ever been treated for drug use, or is considered likely to deliver a baby prematurely.

Private investigators can find even more, tapping into commercial databases, government records, and even law-enforcement files that, theoretically, should be inaccessible to civilians. It is remarkably easy and inexpensive. With less than $50, a writer for the on-line publication CNET found that a complete stranger (or disgruntled employee, or ex-lover) could obtain a wealth of personal data with only a fax machine and connection to the Net. Within minutes he found his "target's" phone

> *"Modern life is crisscrossed and bound by a web of data that continues to grow in scope and tighten its grip on privacy."*

number and home address; with minimal effort he found her e-mail address, where she worked, where she went to school, memberships in organizations, and newsgroup postings. For only $30, he was able to find her Social Security number; for another $16, he found her credit report. Using a faked signature (actually signed by the willing "target"), the reporter was granted entry to her complete credit history, including the numbers of all her credit cards. For another $200, he could have accessed her bank balance. Even the superrich are vulnerable. CNET also easily found the Social Security numbers of such business moguls as Time Warner Vice Chairman Ted Turner, and Microsoft cofounder Paul Allen. And that was only the start of what could have been discovered.

Professional (and even amateur) investigators are faced with an embarrassment of virtual riches as they snoop into your life because modern life is crisscrossed and bound by a web of data that continues to grow in scope and tighten its grip on privacy. In less than three minutes, subscribers to a service provided by DBT-Online can get the Social Security number, date of birth, and telephone number of any person. Subscribers to the service, known as "Faces of the Nation," reportedly include journalists, as well as bill collectors, insurance companies, and private eyes. Another information broker, CBD Infotek, advertises that it has 1,600 databases covering more than three and a half billion public records.

One detective agency, known as "The Cat," advertises, as one of its services, background checks of potential employees or business partners, but also of someone "you're dating or engaged to," and "nuisance neighbors." The detectives will search for voter, marriage, driving and court records, as well as search for probate and real estate sources. They claim:

> We use advancing state-of-the-art technology, strategies and resources to help you discover "Just the Facts" about your subject's background. We can discover marriages, divorces, former addresses, current and previous employment

verification, references and developed reference checks, credit reports (for permissible purposes only), bankruptcies, check nationwide for outstanding criminal warrants, and the list goes on and on! . . . Unusual requests . . . Please Inquire.

Among the techniques the agency suggests to someone interested in probing someone's background are surprising the person at home during an "unexpected time like the evening or on the weekend. This will definitely give an idea how this person 'really' lives." The agency also suggests checking out the glove compartment of their cars, hitting the redial buttons on a person's phones, and checking out their monthly bank statement or credit-card bill—"This is most interesting reading around or shortly after a holiday (St. Valentine's Day?)."

It is also easy enough to track when and where some people travel. Blending data provided by the government with information on the Internet, snoops can easily track the comings and goings of the 10,000 or so privately owned airplanes—anywhere in the country. For a small fee, subscribers to on-line services such as The Trip.com and Dimensions International can quickly find out where any corporate plane is located, where it is going, and when it is scheduled to arrive. Though such information has been in the public domain for several years, it became available on the Internet only in 1997, when the Federal Aviation Administration approved the release of the information on the net, thus enabling the plane's owners—along with anyone else so inclined—to track their airplanes.

Government and Private Databases

Given the ubiquity of the dataweb, the only way to avoid being included in the databases is to not be born. Government records follow us literally from cradle to grave, and much of that information is not only public record, but actually marketed by cash-hungry governments to private brokers.

Few Americans have anything but the vaguest idea how much of their lives is recorded in such data. As Ashley Dunn has noted, for most of us, the erosion of privacy does not seem alarming since "the core of our private lives remains in the physical world." The scattered bits of data in the electronic universe can seem to be "nothing more than the odds and ends of our lives—data lint that only

> *"Government records follow us literally from cradle to grave, and much of that information is . . . marketed by cash-hungry governments to private brokers."*

the perverse would bother collecting." What makes the current attacks on privacy so insidious is the fact that few of us have any idea how those bits of lint are being gathered into a lint ball of truly remarkable dimensions. "I see this material as junk," Dunn notes, "no closer to a representation of my true soul than the Vatican trash can is of Catholicism. But the point is not whether it is true or not. What matters is that those who collect and use the information accept this gangling ball of lint as truth. *In these computers, we are what the data says we are."*

Not only do we not know how much of this information is out there, or who has it, but we also have only a very slim chance of being able to assure that it is accurate and almost no control over who might have access to it, including insurance companies, creditors, employers, journalists, government investigators, or ex-spouses. What might be included? Everything from your brushes with the law, your school records, bankruptcies, marital problems, whether you have ever had a sexually transmitted disease, or an abortion, your student loan status, your political and religious affiliations, salary, whether you are taking Prozac or Viagra, and your taste in Web sites are potential bits of recoverable data.

Every piece of information has a price: Using 1997 prices, your salary and consumer credit report can be obtained from an information broker for $75; your stock, bond, and mutual-fund records for $200. For $450, brokers can obtain your credit-card number; for $80 to $200 they can put their hands on your telephone records. Your personal medical history for the last ten years is for sale for $400. Not all of this information can be obtained ethically, or even legally. But it *can* be obtained from what *New York Times* reporter Nina Bernstein called the "thriving gray-black market in purloined privacy." There is nothing new about private eyes or snooping, of course, but technology has transformed both the capabilities and the threats. Ever-more-powerful computers and the proliferation of government and private databases make it infinitely easier to access all of this information. Records that had once sat in the backrooms of remote courthouses are now available at the touch of a button. More important, however, the new technologies make possible extraordinary links and mergers of information that can be used to compile detailed dossiers. As Carole Lane remarks, "once information is entered into a database, it takes on a strange new life of its own. . . ."

All signs indicate that the information pool will continue to grow. Governments are making tens of millions of dollars selling public records to junk mailers and other businesses. What efforts have been made to curtail the flow of personal information have been halfhearted, at best. In 1994, after actress Rebecca Schaeffer was murdered by a stalker in 1989 who had obtained her home address through California's driver-license registry, Congress passed a law forbidding states from releasing such personal information as addresses and Social Security numbers. But the law left gaping loopholes: It exempted government agencies, tow-truck operators, junk mailers, and private detectives. In effect, the ban on releasing information applied only to private citizens. In an irony that escaped lawmakers, the new law would not have protected Miss Schaeffer, since her killer had obtained her address from a private detective—who is still entitled to obtain such data under the law.

Among the richest sources of personal information are the handful of super credit bureaus, including TRW, Equifax, and Trans Union, which reportedly maintain files on 90 percent of all American adults. Although they claim to be zealous guardians of the information in those files, the bureaus routinely sell information to employers, landlords, insurance companies, and any business offering credit. Several years ago, *Business Week* tested the bureaus, obtaining detailed credit reports on magazine employees for a mere $20 apiece. For a $500 initial fee, the magazine's writers were able to access the bureaus' databases from their home computers. They were not only able to check colleagues for $15 a shot, but were able to snoop into the credit files of several well-known individuals, including then–Vice President Dan Quayle.

Privacy Violations

All of this is purely theoretical, until it hits home. Even if you understand the scope and breadth and ease with which your life can be dissected, the reality can still come as a considerable shock. The reality of violation is quite different from the *idea* of violation; it is the difference between reading a newspaper article about crime and coming home to find your house trashed by burglars.

One day after I had been working on this book for more than a year, and had written much of the preceding chapter, an investigative reporter for a local newspaper dropped off a sealed manila envelope. Inside were the results of a quick background check into . . . me. On the front page of the packet was my Social Security number, my date of birth, my home phone number, my driver's license number, the assessed value of my house, how much I paid for it, along with every address I had lived in for the past decade.

But it did not stop there.

By running a single cheek, the reporter had found both my wife's and my daughter's Social Security numbers and drivers' license numbers. There was also my college-age daughter's address at college and her home phone number. The dossier listed my father's Social Security number and the month and year of his death. The service to which the reporter subscribed offered other information as well: It cast a web that captured almost everyone around me. The names, addresses, and phone numbers of every one of my neighbors was listed. There was the Social Security number of the people who bought my old house, along with every address they had had in the past decade. I also now have the Social Security numbers of the couple from whom I purchased my current house. I know everywhere *they* have lived for the past three decades.

> *"What efforts have been made to curtail the flow of personal information have been halfhearted, at best."*

But there was more.

Because the scan had also picked up my workplace, the dataweb snared nearly two dozen of my coworkers, printing out the dates of birth, Social Security numbers, home addresses, and past addresses of people with whom I had the merest nodding acquaintance. Intriguingly, some of the company's management—and their spouses—fell into the dragnet. I confess I more than half-enjoyed walking into their offices and reading off their information—including addresses they had long forgotten, watching for their reactions. Information is power. It is also profoundly unsettling.

Public Outcry

The public got a taste of the brave new world of datawebs in 1996, when Lexis-Nexis, one of the country's best-known research companies, announced that it would provide a new tracking service with access to hundreds of millions of Social Security numbers. The company boasted that its product, known as P-TRAK Personal Locator, "puts 300 million names right at your fingertips." With a few keystrokes, the system would provide "a quick, convenient search [that] provides up to three addresses, as well as aliases, maiden names, and Social Security numbers." The announcement highlighted the fact that while the government was limited in the ways it could use Social Security numbers, there were no restrictions on their use by private companies, like Lexis-Nexis. Specifically, Lexis-Nexis was targeting lawyers, corporations, investigators, law-enforcement officials, librarians, and journalists who might subscribe to the service. Almost immediately, privacy concerns were raised about the new service, including fears that the service left individuals vulnerable to fraud or even the theft of their identities by someone with access to their Social Security numbers. Initially, Lexis-Nexis brushed off such concerns, saying it was not responsible for what happened to the information it would send out. "Our company's policy has been, and continues to be, that this product is to be used in a legal manner and that's one thing that we try to stress with our customers," an executive said. "If something did happen, we wouldn't deal with it because we are a third party."

Such insouciance did little to calm critics, and after an onslaught of criticism and complaints—much of it generated through the Internet—the company dropped the service after only ten days. Although the case has been widely cited as a victory of privacy advocates, the fact is that the information offered by P-TRAK is still readily available on the Net and through information brokers. Privacy advocates had won another Pyrrhic victory in the early 1990s, after the Lotus Corporation unveiled a new marketing product known as "Marketplace: Households," a CD-ROM with data on the buying practices and incomes of 120 million Americans. Faced with public outcry, the CD-ROM was withdrawn, but again, the victory was only partial. As David Brin notes, "[I]ronically, Marketplace would only have provided the same access for small business that big companies already enjoy."

The trend seems to be accelerating, driven not only by technology and the private market in information, but also by rather dramatic expansions of government databases. Perhaps the most extraordinary is the National Directory of New Hires, and workers' database, which were created as part of immigration and welfare-reform legislation. Ostensibly designed to facilitate the enforcement of child-support orders, the New Hires directory is a massive computerized tracking system that will include every person hired by every employer in the country. Beginning October 1, 1997, private employers are required by law to tell the government the names, addresses, Social Security numbers, and wages of every new employee, creating one of the most extensive "data dragnets" in history.

Reflecting the apparently inexhaustible appetite of federal agencies for personal information, in 1998 the nation's banking regulators proposed new rules that would, in effect, require banks and savings and loans to spy on their customers. Dubbed the "Know Your Customer Rule," the proposal by the Federal Deposit Insurance Corporation (FDIC) and other agencies would have required banks to "develop a program designed to determine the identity of its customers, determine its customer's sources of funds; determine the normal and expected transactions of its customers; monitor account activity for transactions that are inconsistent with those normal and expected transactions; and report any transactions of its customers that are determined to be suspicious."

News of the proposal generated widespread outrage and opposition from some bankers' groups. "We think the regulation is by its very nature, at odds with attempts to protect customer privacy," said Paul Stock of the North Carolina Bankers Association. Ostensibly, the rule was intended to "reduce the likelihood that [banks] will become unwitting participants in illicit activities" such as money laundering and drug trafficking by flagging out-of-the-ordinary withdrawal or deposits. But the rule did not apply simply to customers who were under suspicion—it applied to *every* customer at *every* bank. Defending the proposal, the FDIC insisted that any such system "should respect the private nature of the relationship that customers have with their financial institutions." But the entire point of the regulation is that the relationship is *not* private. On the contrary, it effectively deputized the nation's banks to act as agents of federal law-enforcement agencies, by requiring them to maintain detailed dossiers and profiles on their own customers. Banks would not only have to learn where each customer's money came from, but would have to keep surreptitious watch on every deposit and withdrawal and blow the whistle to the feds whenever a customer deviated from the norm. By dramatically extending the reach of federal agents into our bank accounts, the proposed rule marked yet another step toward the criminalization of society, in which average citizens are now subject to the kind of scrutiny and surveillance—from fingerprinting to video monitoring—once reserved for criminal suspects. Indeed, no society has ever been watched as carefully as ours.

Stronger Privacy Protection Laws Are Necessary

by Dianne Feinstein

About the author: *Dianne Feinstein is the senior U.S. senator from California.*

[In June 2001] Americans were inundated by letter upon letter from banks, credit-card companies, and other financial institutions explaining their privacy policies. Why? So that these companies could comply with the July 1, 2001, deadline as required by the 1999 Gramm-Leach-Bliley banking deregulation law.

Most people, however, threw these notices in the trash. The material was confusing and often disregarded. But if you didn't take the notice seriously, the company may be free to sell your personal information to anyone willing to buy it.

Identity Piracy: A Growing Problem

Put simply, the 1999 law didn't go far enough to protect Americans' personal information. As a result, people are more at risk from identity theft than ever before.

Increasingly, your personal information—such as Social Security number, driver's license, and health and financial data—can be purchased without your knowledge for as little as $35 on the Internet or by pilfering your trash or mail. The FBI estimates that a case of identity theft occurs every two minutes, or roughly 350,000 times each year. Additionally, the Social Security Administration reports that misuse of Social Security numbers has grown 500% in only four years.

Identity piracy can happen to anyone—even a prosecutor. Recently, a Colorado assistant attorney general had no idea that her identity had been stolen until she received a call from Sprint regarding three accounts for cellular phone service she hadn't set up. The thieves stole her Social Security number, birth date, address, and other information to run up $5,086 worth of charges in her name. Like thousands of other victims, she was forced to spend countless hours attempting to restore her good name and credit rating after collection agents didn't believe she was a victim.

Another example of identity piracy was uncovered recently when the U.S. Secret Service busted an identity-theft ring in Orange County, California, that used the names of 1,500 people nationwide to steal nearly $2 million.

> *"What's needed is a comprehensive level of [privacy] protection."*

The loss of privacy, however, has more than an economic cost. People have a right to be left alone and to keep the most intimate details of their lives to themselves. Just think of the serious harm that can be done if one's health status, religious affiliation, or spending habits are cavalierly exposed to the public eye.

We must ask ourselves: Are we doing enough to protect people from this growing crime? After trying to decipher the recent bevy of privacy notices, I would hazard a guess that most Americans would say no.

Comprehensive Privacy Protection

The problem is that many of the measures pending before Congress today provide only part of the solution. What's needed is a comprehensive level of protection.

I have legislation to do just that, striking a balance between the personal right of privacy and the needs of legitimate commerce. The bill puts strict protections on Americans' most sensitive personal information. The measure also prevents companies from being able to sell Social Security numbers to the general public. And in a major change from current law, this bill requires that a company can sell a person's financial data, health data, or driver's license information only with the individual's explicit permission. The requirement of affirmative consent is also known as "opt-in."

I realize that we live in a high-technology society where, in many cases, information is the currency of commerce. All of us demand the convenience of instant credit and online transactions; if businesses can't share this information, some of these conveniences are put at risk. Therefore, the bill also lets companies sell nonsensitive information such as addresses and phone numbers. But companies must give individuals a reasonable opportunity to withhold this information if they so choose. In other words, individuals can choose to opt out of the transaction.

The bottom line is that the balance between privacy and commerce is sometimes a difficult one. But it can be done. We shouldn't let the status quo remain when it comes to privacy.

I'm struck by a speech that British playwright George Bernard Shaw gave in New York in 1933 in which he said, "An American has no sense of privacy. He does not know what it means. There is no such thing in the country."

Let's prove him wrong. As the use of personal information in our society continues to escalate, we must ensure that our privacy laws keep pace with that growth.

Editor's note: As of June 2002, the privacy protection bill Senator Feinstein describes was still before Congress.

Individuals' Ability to Communicate Anonymously Via the Internet Is Threatened

by Jonathan D. Wallace

About the author: *Jonathan D. Wallace is an attorney and the author of* Sex, Law, and Cyberspace: Freedom and Censorship on the Frontiers of the Online Revolution.

In a 1997 decision, a Federal district court in Georgia invalidated a state law criminalizing anonymous and pseudonymous Internet communications. In so doing, the court issued a decision consistent with centuries of American tradition and jurisprudence. Throughout the history of the U.S., pseudonymous and anonymous authors have made a rich contribution to political discourse. Had the court held any other way, it would have fallen into the common trap of treating the Internet as being unique, unrelated to any prior communications media. Instead, the court recognized that there is no distinction to be drawn between anonymous communications on the Net and in a leaflet or book.

The Rich Tradition of Anonymous Speech

Controversial and thought-provoking speech has frequently been issued from under the cover of anonymity, by writers who feared prosecution or worse if their identities were known. The authors of Cato's Letters, an influential series of essays about freedom of speech and political liberty published from 1720 on, were two British men, John Trenchard and Thomas Gordon. Cato's Letters had a wide following in America.

In 1735, printer John Peter Zenger was arrested for seditious libel for publishing pseudonymous essays by Lewis Morris, James Alexander, and others attacking New York Governor William Cosby. Zenger also republished several of

Cato's Letters. Andrew Hamilton defended Zenger. In his stirring oration to the jury, he asked them to lay "a foundation for securing to ourselves, our posterity, and our neighbors" the right of "exposing and opposing arbitrary power . . . by speaking and writing truth." The jury's acquittal of Zenger helped to end prosecutions of American writers and publishers under British common law.

Thomas Paine's *Common Sense*, acclaimed as the work which sparked Americans to think about separating from Britain, was first published signed simply "An Englishman." Alexander Hamilton, John Jay, and James Madison wrote *The Federalist Papers* under the joint pseudonym "Publius."

Pseudonymity continued to play an important role in political speech in the 20th century. George Kennan, a high-ranking member of General George Marshall and President Harry Truman's staff, considered by many to be the architect of America's policy of "containment," signed his influential 1947 essay, "The Sources of Soviet Power," merely as "X." Politicians, including presidents, communicate anonymously with the media when they wish to express ideas or disseminate information without attribution, and press reports are full of quotes attributed to sources such as "a senior State Department official" or a "senior White House staff member." Pseudonymity has also protected people stigmatized by prior political speech or association; many blacklisted writers continued to work throughout the McCarthy era by using names other than their own.

Protected by the First Amendment

The Supreme Court has consistently held that anonymous and pseudonymous speech is protected by the First Amendment. In 1995, in *McIntyre v. Ohio Campaign Commission*, the Court invalidated an Ohio ordinance requiring the authors of campaign leaflets to identify themselves. McIntyre had been fined for handing out anonymous leaflets during a local school board campaign. The Court repeated what it had said in a prior case: "Anonymous pamphlets, leaflets, brochures and even books have played an important role in the progress of mankind." It recognized that authors may have a variety of valid motives for shielding their identity, including fear of retaliation.

The Court placed McIntyre's leaflet in the context of centuries of anonymous political discourse: "Under our Constitution, anonymous pamphleteering is not a pernicious, fraudulent practice, but an honorable tradition of advocacy and of dissent.

> *"The Supreme Court has consistently held that anonymous and pseudonymous speech is protected by the First Amendment."*

Anonymity is a shield from the tyranny of the majority." Although the Supreme Court usually refers only to prior case law and scholarly legal writings in its holdings, the justices took the unusual measure of citing John Stuart

Mill's *On Liberty* in support of the proposition that anonymity is a protection against the majority's tyranny.

The parallel between McIntyre's leaflet and an unsigned Web page or e-mail on a political topic is obvious. Nevertheless, people who fail to see the analogy between the Internet and print media continue to call for a ban on anonymity in cyberspace.

In 1996, the Georgia legislature passed H.B. 1630, an amendment to the state's Computer Systems Protection Act, making it a misdemeanor for one "knowingly to transmit any data through a computer network [using] any individual name . . . to falsely identify the person . . . transmitting such data. . . .

"Immediately, a group of plaintiffs including the American Civil Liberties Union and the author of this article brought suit in Federal district court in Georgia challenging the constitutionality of the law. The district court granted a preliminary injunction against enforcement of the act, holding that "the statute's prohibition of Internet transmissions which 'falsely identify' the sender constitutes a presumptively invalid content-based restriction" under *McIntyre*.

The court concluded that the statute was vague and overbroad because it was "not drafted with the precision necessary for laws regulating speech. On its face, the act prohibits such protected speech as the use of false identification to avoid social ostracism, to prevent discrimination and harassment, and to protect privacy . . . a prohibition with well-recognized first amendment problems." The preliminary injunction was later converted into a permanent one, and the state of Georgia decided not to make an appeal, so the district court's ruling became the final and definitive statement on H.B. 1630.

Implications for the Internet

"The ultimate implication, I believe, is that to achieve a civilized form of cyberspace, we have to limit the use of anonymous communications," David Johnson wrote in "The Unscrupulous Diner's Dilemma and Anonymity in Cyberspace." In a *Columbia Law Review* note published in October, 1996, Noah Levine called for "a simple statute . . . requiring administrators of anonymous remailers to maintain records of users in a manner which allows for the identification of senders of specific messages." Levine, like most commentators on this side of the issue, failed to say why *McIntyre* would not apply in cyberspace.

The Supreme Court said in *Reno v. ACLU* that, "Through the use of Web pages, mail exploders and newsgroups, [any Net user] can become a pamphleteer." As the Court recognized, a Web page is an electronic leaflet. However, if proponents of Internet anonymity legislation have their way, the same text may be treated differently depending on whether it is printed on paper or stored in electronic form. These proponents, therefore, incur a responsibility to explain why Internet communications are to be treated differently than print communications.

There are a limited number of legal theories that advocates of regulation have used to justify such treatment, and the two most important ones have already been rejected by the Supreme Court. Radio and broadcast television have been more tightly regulated than print media based on a theory of "spectrum scarcity," while a "pervasiveness" doctrine first raised in *F.C.C. v. Pacifica* (the "seven dirty words" case) has been used to justify the regulation of speech disseminated both by broadcast and cable media. While no one can reasonably argue that the Net is a "scarce" medium, proponents of Internet censorship relied very heavily on the argument that it is "pervasive," meaning that it comes into the house and may present speech inappropriate for minors. In 1999, in affirming the unconstitutionality of the Communications Decency Act, the Supreme Court decisively held that the Internet is not "scarce": "The Internet can hardly be considered a 'scarce' expressive commodity. It provides relatively unlimited, low-cost capacity for communications of all kinds." Nor is it a "pervasive" medium under *Pacifica:* "The Internet is not as 'invasive' as radio or television."

> *"Legislators should be . . . wary of laws that require sweeping changes to communications technology in order to serve speech-restricting goals."*

Another argument sometimes raised by proponents of Internet speech regulation is even less supported by case law—that marginal speech on the Net is more dangerous than the same speech in print because it reaches larger audiences more easily. The proposition that controversial speech is acceptable so long as it only reaches a very few listeners flies directly in the face of the governing metaphor of First Amendment jurisprudence, as stated by Justice Oliver Wendell Holmes: "The ultimate good desired is better reached by free trade in ideas . . . the best test of truth is the power of the thought to get itself accepted in the competition of the market." Proponents of regulation, by contrast, argue that government must intervene whenever controversial speech is about to gain acceptance in the marketplace of ideas.

A closely related argument is that anonymous speech is more dangerous on the Internet because of the lack of gatekeepers, such as publishers, editors, or television producers who may know the identity of the anonymous speaker or filter out anonymous speech. However, this argument is highly antidemocratic and opposed to free markets, because it presupposes that anonymous speech is acceptable only if prescreened by an informed elite. No gatekeeper stood between McIntyre and her intended audience.

Since the Georgia decision, law enforcement authorities have continued to call for the elimination of anonymity on the Internet. On December 17, 1997, law enforcement officials from the U.S. and seven other industrialized countries issued a joint statement calling for "information and telecommunications systems" to be "designed to help prevent and detect network abuse." They said it would be "helpful to law enforcement if . . . packets [sent over the Internet] would transmit information reliably as to where they came from, including user and service provider." A few months later, FBI Director Louis Freeh testified to a Senate subcommittee: "It would be beneficial for law enforcement if Internet service providers [retain] subscriber information and records for screen names and associated . . . 'IP addresses.'"

Preserve Anonymous Speech on the Internet

Laws requiring the disclosure of identity in cyberspace would necessitate far-reaching changes in Internet technology. Today, one can set up an Internet account without one's full name being stored anywhere on the Internet. In fact, by setting up an account on a private network attached to the Internet, users may gain use of the Net without placing their identity on file anywhere at all. Anonymity and pseudonymity are built into the architecture of the Net. Legislators should be particularly wary of laws that require sweeping changes to communications technology in order to serve speech-restricting goals.

Anonymous and pseudonymous speech on the Internet forms a part of the rich tradition of such speech in other media, including print, and is entitled to the same First Amendment protections. Legislation against anonymity threatens to end that rich tradition, and should be opposed.

Face-Recognition Technology Threatens Individual Privacy

by Jay Stanley and Barry Steinhardt

About the authors: *Jay Stanley is the privacy public education coordinator at the American Civil Liberties Union and a former analyst at Forrester Research. Barry Steinhardt is associate director of the ACLU, chair of the ACLU Cyberliberties Task Force, and cofounder of the Global Internet Liberty Campaign.*

Since September 11, facial recognition systems—computer programs that analyze images of human faces gathered by video surveillance cameras—are being increasingly discussed and occasionally deployed, largely as a means for combating terrorism. They are being set up in several airports around the United States, including Logan Airport in Boston, T.F. Green Airport in Providence, Rhode Island, San Francisco International Airport, Fresno Airport in California and Palm Beach International Airport in Florida. The technology was also used at the 2001 Super Bowl, and plans are underway to use it at the NFL championship again in 2002.

The technology is not just being used in places where terrorists are likely to strike, however: in Tampa, Florida, it is also being aimed at citizens on public streets. In the summer of 2001, the Tampa Police Department installed several dozen cameras, assigned staff to monitor them, and installed a face recognition application called Face-IT® manufactured by the Visionics Corporation of New Jersey. On June 29, 2001, the department began scanning the faces of citizens as they walked down Seventh Avenue in the Ybor City neighborhood.

Acting under a Florida open-records law, the ACLU was able to obtain all existing police logs filled out by the operators of the city's face recognition system in July and August, 2001. Those documents and logs reveal several important things about the technology in one of its first real-world trials:

- The system has never correctly identified a single face in its database of suspects, let alone resulted in any arrests.

- The system was suspended on August 11, 2001, and has not been in operation since.
- In the brief period before the department discontinued the keeping of a log, the system made many false positives, including such errors as confusing what were to a human easily identifiable male and female images.
- The photographic database contains a broader selection of the population than just criminals wanted by the police, including such people as those who might have "valuable intelligence" for the police or who have criminal records.

The Problems with Facial Recognition Technology

Facial recognition systems are built on computer programs that analyze images of human faces for the purpose of identifying them. The programs take a facial image, measure characteristics such as the distance between the eyes, the length of the nose, and the angle of the jaw, and create a unique file called a "template." Using templates, the software then compares that image with another image—such as a photograph in a database of criminals—and produces a score that measures how similar the images are to each other. The software operator sets a threshold score above which the system sets off an alarm for a possible match.

One potential problem with such a powerful surveillance system is that experience tells us it will inevitably be abused. Video camera systems are operated by humans, who after all bring to the job all their existing prejudices and biases. In Great Britain, which has experimented with the widespread installation of closed circuit video cameras in public places, camera operators have been found to focus dis-

> *"[Florida's face recognition] system has never correctly identified a single face in its database of suspects."*

proportionately on people of color; and the mostly male (and probably bored) operators frequently focus voyeuristically on women.

An investigation by the *Detroit Free Press* also shows the kind of abuses that can take place when police are given unregulated access to powerful surveillance tools. Examining how a database available to Michigan law enforcement was used, the newspaper found that officers had used it to help their friends or themselves stalk women, threaten motorists, track estranged spouses—even to intimidate political opponents. The unavoidable truth is that surveillance tools will inevitably be abused.

Facial recognition is particularly subject to abuse because it can be used in a passive way that doesn't require the knowledge, consent, or participation of subjects. It is possible to put a camera up anywhere and train it on people; modern cameras can easily view faces from over 100 yards away. People act differently when they are being watched, and have the right to know if their movements and identities are being captured. "I've seen it all," Tampa-police camera operator Raymond C. Green told the *St. Petersburg Times.* "Some things are really funny, like the way people dance when they think no one's looking. Others, you wouldn't want to watch."

This technology has the potential to become an extremely intrusive, privacy-invasive part of American life. History shows that once installed, this kind of a surveillance system rarely remains confined to its original purpose. Already, in the case of face recognition, it has spread from purportedly looking for terrorists at the high-profile Super Bowl to searching for petty criminals and runaways on the public streets of Tampa.

> *"[Facial recognition] technology has the potential to become an extremely intrusive, privacy-invasive part of American life."*

Given the problematic social consequences of going down the path of widespread deployment of facial recognition–enabled video surveillance systems, proponents of the technology must at least demonstrate that it will be highly effective in achieving the goal for which it is being justified: combating terrorism and other crimes. However, all prior indications have been that the technology is not effective and does not work very well. Two separate government studies have found that it performed poorly even under ideal conditions where subjects are staring directly into the camera under bright lights. Several government agencies have abandoned facial recognition systems after finding they did not work as advertised, including the Immigration and Naturalization Service, which experimented with using the technology to identify people in cars at the Mexico-US border. And the well-known security consultant Richard Smith, experimenting with FaceIT®—the same package used by the Tampa police—found that it was easily tripped up by changes in lighting, in the quality of the camera used, in the angle from which a face was photographed, in facial expression, in the composition of the background of a photograph, and by the donning of sunglasses or even regular glasses.

The ACLU Investigation of Tampa's Facial Recognition System

Because facial recognition is such a potentially powerful and invasive surveillance tool and because the Tampa police department's deployment represents one of the first real-world tests of facial recognition technology, the ACLU was eager for details on the system and how it was being used. On August 2, 2001, the ACLU of Florida filed a request under Florida's open-records law (the state equivalent of the federal Freedom of Information Act) for all documents pertaining to:

- the decision-making process by which Tampa elected to deploy the system
- camera locations
- the technical capabilities of the system being used

- the procedures, instructions and training provided to system operators
- the contents of the image databases
- written procedures for how the identification process is handled
- future plans for these systems

A second request was submitted on October 19, 2001. A third letter was sent to the department on November 27.

On December 4, the ACLU was furnished with copies of police logs filled in by system operators between July 12 and August 11, 2001; a Memorandum of Understanding between the software manufacturer, Visionics, and the police department; the department's Standard Operating Procedure governing the use of the system; and a training video.

The Results: No Hits, No Arrests, Many False Positives

The Tampa Police Department Face-IT® operator logs obtained by the ACLU show that the system not only has not produced a single arrest, but it also has not resulted in the correct identification of a single person from the department's photo database on the sidewalks of Tampa. Tampa police Detective Bill Todd not only confirmed these results to the ACLU in phone conversations on December 17–18, but he also acknowledged that the system has been out of operation since the last log sheet was filled in on August 11.

The earliest logs provided by the department show activity for July 12, 13, 14, and 20, 2001. On those dates, the system operators logged 14 instances in which the system indicated a possible match. Of the 14 matches on those four days, all were false alarms. Two of the "matches" were of the opposite sex from the person in the database, and three others were ruled out by the monitoring officers due to differences in age, weight or other characteristics that made the mismatch obvious to a human observer. The rest of the false positives were simply noted with a terse "not subject." These results are consistent with an anecdotal report in the July 19, 2001 *St. Petersburg Times* that "the alarm sounds an average of five times each night."

After July 20, 2001, the remaining logs provided by the department are blank, and no logs were provided for dates later than August 11. Based on conversations with representatives of the Tampa Police, it appears that the blank logs are attributable to one of two possibilities or a combination of those possibilities:

- Because of the high number of false positives, the department changed the software's "threshold" setting that determines how firm a match is required before an alarm is sounded. That change resulted in far fewer false positives (but would have also further reduced the chances that anyone in the database who wandered in front of the department's cameras would actually be identified by the software).
- Acting either on their own or at the direction of an internal policy decision, the officers operating the system decided to record only genuine matches,

and not false positives. The log sheets are blank because there were no genuine matches.

Because the system does not automatically scan the faces of people on the sidewalks—operators must manually zoom in on a citizen's face before it registers in the software—it would not be surprising that system operators faced with an endless string of negative results would spend less and less time and energy searching out and capturing facial images, as opposed to simply watching the video images for signs of trouble.

A reporter for the *St. Petersburg Times* reported on July 19 that on the night he visited—at the apparent peak of the system's operation—the operator captured 457 faces out of the estimated 125,000 people who visit Ybor City on a typical Friday. If that proportion were to decline further, the already tiny chances for obtaining a genuine match with a photo in the database would shrink even more.

Detective Todd explained the lack of any log sheets after August 11 by confirming that the Face-IT® system was taken out of service. (A notation of "N/A" on the August 11 log sheet may have indicated that the system was used only for a test or demonstration that day, he said.) Todd explained the decision as a result of a police redistricting, which necessitated training new officers in the system's operation. He said that the department planned to resume use of the system at some point in the future. However, it is reasonable to assume that the professionals in the Tampa PD would not have let the system sit unused for so long because of a mere redistricting process had they previously found facial recognition to be a valuable tool in the effort to combat crime.

> *"[Facial recognition] technology does not deliver security benefits sufficient to justify the Orwellian dangers that [it presents]."*

One Nation, Under Suspicion?

The department's written guidelines for "Utilization of Face-IT® Software" reveal several other interesting points about Tampa's use of face recognition. First, the guidelines state that photographs are entered into the database if the subjects are wanted by the police; if "it is determined that valuable intelligence can be gathered from contact" with a person; or "based upon an individual's prior criminal activity and record."

"Twenty percent of the criminals commit 80 percent of the crimes," the guidelines state. "It is the intention of the Tampa Police Department to identify those subjects through the use of this software. Through this proactive approach, the Tampa Police Department can deter criminal activity prior to a criminal offense being committed."

Far from protecting citizens against the next terrorist strike or other violent crimes, the department's guidelines thus make clear that the system was used in an attempt to assist the full range of cases in which local police are involved. Not just terrorists and violent criminals, but anyone who might have "valuable intelligence" for the cop on the beat, according to these guidelines, will have his or her photograph entered into a police database so that they may set off an alarm whenever they visit a public place that is within the lens of a department camera.

The move to permanently brand some people as "under suspicion" and monitor them as they move about in public places has deep and significant social ramifications. If we are to take that path—a step that the ACLU opposes—we should do so as a nation, consciously, after full debate and discussion, and not simply slide down that road through the incremental actions of local police departments.

Vast Potential for Abuse

The documentary record obtained by the ACLU of the Tampa Police Department's experience with facial recognition technology adds an important new piece of evidence that the technology does not deliver security benefits sufficient to justify the Orwellian dangers that they present. What the logs show—and fail to show—tells us that face recognition software performs at least as badly in real-world conditions as it has in the more controlled experiments that have been carried out.

The only possible justification for deploying such an ineffective technology would be that it somehow deters crime because citizens believe that it works. There are several problems with that argument. First, it is premised on a Wizard of Oz–style strategy of hiding the truth about facial recognition technology from the public—a stance that is not compatible with the vital importance of public scrutiny of the tools, technologies and techniques that police departments deploy.

Second, even if face recognition cameras did deter wanted criminals from frequenting the areas under surveillance, all that would happen is that the criminals would move to other locations. Indeed, sociological studies of closed circuit television monitoring of public places in Britain—where residents are widely aware of the cameras—have shown that it has not succeeded in reducing crime.

Given the system's poor performance in Tampa—which the police department there has implicitly recognized in their decision to stop actively using it—the ACLU hopes that police departments around the nation will step back, objectively examine the costs and benefits of the system, and reject them as ineffective. Other cities have voted to deploy these systems, including Virginia Beach, Palm Springs and Boulder City, Nevada. We ask those cities to consider the documentary evidence from Tampa and not waste precious resources on this illusory path toward public safety.

The worst-case scenario would be if police continue to utilize facial recognition systems despite their ineffectiveness because they become invested in them, attached to government or industry grants that support them, or begin to discover additional, even more frightening uses for the technology. The continued use of facial recognition technology under these circumstances would divert limited law enforcement resources from more productive pursuits, create a dangerous false sense of security, and ultimately threaten the privacy, freedom and safety of everyone in America.

The Threat to Privacy Is Exaggerated

by Michael Lind

About the author: *Michael Lind is a senior fellow at the New America Foundation, a nonprofit public policy institute, and the coauthor of* The Radical Center: The Future of American Politics.

In a remarkably short period of time, "privacy" has moved from the margins to the center of political debate in the United States, Canada and Europe. The nebulous concept today embraces a number of issues, ranging from the serious—the possible abuse of the results of genetic testing by corporations and the government—to the trivial—the sharing of information about consumer preferences among businesses that bombard hapless consumers with unsolicited catalogs and e-mail advertisements. What unites these diverse concerns, according to the emerging consensus, is the danger that new technologies of surveillance, data-recording and data exchange will be put to nefarious purposes. Big Brother, we are cautioned again and again, is finally here—not in the form of a totalitarian state, but of something subtler and perhaps more sinister, a universal surveillance society.

A few thinkers have challenged this perception, among them the communitarian sociologist Amitai Etzioni, who stresses the need to balance individual privacy against the legitimate interests of the community, and the scientist David Brin, who argues that we must adapt to "the transparent society" rather than attempt to prevent its evolution. Despite these dissenters, fear of the imminent erosion of a historic right, and of a threatening new, soft totalitarianism, is rapidly becoming the conventional wisdom. It strikes me as not only nonsense, but dangerous nonsense that could do enormous harm to a great many people.

A Simplistic View

The idea that there was a golden age of personal privacy in the past is naive. Until a few generations ago, most Americans lived on farms or in small towns or crowded neighborhoods where personal privacy, in the contemporary sense, was virtually nonexistent. This was as true of the aristocrat, surrounded most of the time by servants, as it was of the peasant sharing a one- or two-room hut with family and, sometimes, livestock. In a letter of paternal advice to his son, the 19th-century American architect Henry Hobson Richardson warned that confidences should never be committed to paper, because servants were fond of reading letters. The young William Faulkner, during a stint as a postmaster, is alleged to have amused himself by reading the mail of his neighbors.

In the era of the telephone party line, operators were notorious for eavesdropping. A woman who worked for the phone company in the 1940s, when operators on roller skates monitored wall-sized batteries of phone wires, once told me that if an operator picked up a particularly salacious conversation, she would motion to her coworkers and they would roll over to listen. As recently as the John F. Kennedy, Lyndon B. Johnson and Richard M. Nixon administrations, the FBI seems to have been wiretapping anyone of any prominence in the United States.

Searching for a constitutional pedigree for their campaign, privacy crusaders in the United States have merely been able to come up with a few tidbits—a quote from Justice Louis D. Brandeis here, an early 20th-century court case about publishing photographs without permission there. The truth is that the notion of privacy in its current elastic sense dates back only to the 1960s and '70s, when it first entered public discourse in connection with reproductive choice in Supreme Court decisions like *Griswold v. Connecticut* (1965) and *Roe v. Wade* (1973). Agglomerating a growing number of distinct controversies and filing all of them under "privacy" is an even later political phenomenon.

It is also the simple and misleading modus operandi of the new privacy theorists: They link together discrete disputes that would best be analyzed separately—for instance, the argument about using biometric cameras to catch criminals, and the question of mandatory HIV testing of newborns. Instead of dealing with each case on its own merits, they retreat to the higher, abstract principle of privacy.

To accept the lumping together of different topics as "aspects" of a single "privacy issue" is to engage in the debate on their terms. Worse, it is to put oneself in the unpopular position of being "against" privacy. The sensible alternative would not only be to treat each situation individually, but

> *"The idea that there was a golden age of personal privacy in the past is naive."*

to recognize personal privacy as just one of several competing factors deserving consideration. This would make it possible to conclude, for example, that corporations should not be allowed to subpoena the PCs of employees to learn whether they are involved in union activity, and that all newborns should be tested for HIV—or the opposite.

An Emotional Issue

Of course, mine is a minority opinion. The claim that a historic right is on the block, putting our democratic society in jeopardy, is ascendant. But if, as I believe, the conventional wisdom about privacy is deeply confused, what explains its appeal to so many otherwise thoughtful people?

The answer, I would suggest, has less to do with politics than sociology. No one who follows the privacy debate with a degree of objectivity can fail to be impressed by two things: Its tone is peculiarly emotional, and its social base is peculiarly elitist. The emotionalism is familiar from past "moral panics," such as the fear of fluoridation or the much-hyped "epidemics" of child-stealing in the 1980s and church-burning in the 1990s, which turned out later to be fabricated from misunderstood data. The fear that the convergence of high technology with law enforcement and business practices is about to rob us of our privacy has all the hallmarks of a classic, irrational moral panic.

This is especially clear where privacy questions intersect with those involving sex and children. In addition, one is struck by a difference in the reactions of men and women (these are my impressions, but I trust that the experience of others bears them out as well). If advances in camera and computer technology are contributing to the salience of the privacy issue in politics, my sense is that—to put it

"The emotional electricity that crackles around the privacy issue comes from fear of public exposure and humiliation."

crudely—women tend to be more obsessed with cameras and men with computers. Women express a disproportionate concern about being objects of male voyeurism. In public discussions of privacy, one hears them repeatedly raise the specter of employers secreting a camera in the women's bathroom. Many of the same women who dread high-tech Peeping Toms, though, appear to be the purchasers of "kindercams" and "nannycams"—the tiny cameras hidden in clocks and other appliances to spy on children and their caretakers.

Men, to judge by their contributions to public discussions of privacy, are less worried about cameras in the bathroom than they are about the boss or the government tracking their surfing on the Web. Furthermore—to make another generalization I believe can be confirmed—this male anxiety is most intense among affluent, college-educated, heterosexuals.

The new privacy crusaders claim they are defending us all against abuses of power by authority. But the groups most likely to suffer from discrimination and exploitation—the working class and poor, members of racial minorities, gays and lesbians—appear to be much less preoccupied with the alleged problem than more mainstream members of the suburban, educated overclass.

The paradox is glaring. The very people who, thanks to their privileged backgrounds, are most likely to be corporate executives and high-level civil servants, tend to be most alarmed about the prospect of corporations and governments being able to acquire information they want to conceal. I have been in rooms full of well-heeled individuals where only one person dissented from the consensus that citizens should be allowed to hide any information they choose from law enforcement agencies by means of encryption devices of the sort used by spies, terrorist organizations and organized crime. I suspect that in a room full of blue-collar workers, a consensus in favor of the law enforcement agencies would be equally pronounced.

There are two possible explanations. One is that the elite—in particular, elite men—know from personal experience how abusive business and government can be, and rationally fear giving employers and government agencies high-tech tools to gather, codify and transmit information. The other possibility is that a lot of people have something to hide. The peculiarly hysterical tone adopted by many otherwise reasonable persons when discussing privacy, then, is easily understandable: They are afraid of being caught.

The second hypothesis brings to mind a remark by the cartoonist Scott Adams, in his book *The Dilbert Future*: "In the future, new technology will allow the police to solve 100 per cent of all crimes. The bad news is that we'll realize 100 per cent of the population are criminals, including the police." The major source of the moral panic that is the privacy scare, I have come to believe, is the apprehension of many Americans that a truly sophisticated system of camera surveillance and computer information collection will catch them doing things that are technically illegal or, if legal, personally embarrassing. The emotional electricity that crackles around the privacy issue comes from fear of public exposure and humiliation.

Public Personas, Private Weaknesses

Every society suffers from the gap between its professed social code and the actual norms of everyday life. Those who try to live strictly according to the code are generally considered annoying prudes; those who openly reject the code are usually treated as probable subversives. Most of us are hypocrites. We pay lip service to the public norms, while frequently flouting them and tolerating considerable deviation in others. Mature, worldly-wise people will look the other way as long as you do not, as the saying goes, frighten the horses.

But the compromise of hypocrisy, in order to succeed, requires a considerable degree of secrecy. (Perhaps the privacy debate should be renamed the secrecy debate.) Once some behavior that is tacitly permitted yet theoretically forbidden is exposed, the public norm is reaffirmed by moral denunciation or at least ridicule of the unfortunate victim.

The catalog of attitudes and actions that are acceptable in secret but unacceptable in public changes constantly. In 1901, illegitimacy or black or Jewish ancestry could be the shocking secret on which a tragic novel turned. In 1951, it was more likely to be homosexuality or a secret divorce. Today's American elite are far more relaxed about all these subjects, to the consternation of conservatives. Nevertheless, the baby boomers and their children have their own morality, and thus their own set of shocking secrets.

It may no longer be disgraceful to have premarital sex, or (in most educated circles) to be homosexual. But the revelation that you are having an extramarital affair, or trolling the Internet for sex partners using the alias Stud Muffin, or perhaps Miss Behavior, would still be highly embarrassing. That alone, I would wager, goes a long way toward explaining the enthusiasm of law-abiding, upright citizens— particularly men—for computer encryption techniques. They are not worried that the FBI or the CIA will discover they are plotting to overthrow the United States. They are worried that their wives will discover their favorite porn sites, or that the FBI agent doing the background check for a Commerce Department job will discover the alias Stud Muffin.

> *"Americans . . . support a privacy regime which would weaken the ability of government to combat terror."*

A similar explanation probably underlies the widespread resistance to the introduction of biometric cameras on street corners and in airports. This is not a tool whose intrinsic value reasonable people can disagree on. Cameras that compare faces to photographs in computer databases are a proven and reliable method of identifying criminals and terrorists. The deployment of 250,000 of them in Great Britain has been an extraordinary success; in Glasgow, Scotland, alone they are credited with reducing crime nearly 70 per cent. Had a proper system of biometric cameras been in place in American airports on September 11, the World Trade Center towers might be standing today.

Why, then, would anyone except a neo-Confederate militiaman in Idaho or a member of the anarchist Left oppose the adoption of so potent a security weapon in the United States? Here, I think, the opposition has to do with the unacknowledged but widespread consumption of recreational drugs—chiefly marijuana, but also cocaine and more exotic substances like heroin and ecstasy. The enormous market for drugs in the U.S. probably includes people most of us would not ever suspect—the secretary, the corporate vice president, the business school professor (perhaps even you, dear reader).

Those respectable secret drug users must live in fear that biometric cameras will photograph them buying drugs from a dealer or a friend in a public place and automatically alert the local vice squad. I have no proof that this accounts for the near panic the device inspires among many individuals who belong to the educated professions and business community. But it seems a reasonable inference, reinforced by the curious lack of alarm about the use of cameras in apartment and office buildings, where no illicit transactions are likely to take place.

The gap between our public personas and our private weaknesses would merely be fodder for sociological analysis or satire or perhaps literary tragedy, if it were not so potentially dangerous. Should enough elite Americans who are afraid of being photographed buying marijuana on a street corner join forces with radical libertarians to prevent the adoption of biometric cameras in public places, an opportunity will be lost to prevent, or punish, many muggings, murders and acts of political terrorism. On a different but no less relevant plane, should enough elite Americans who are afraid of having someone discover their cosmetic surgery or use of Viagra or Prozac lobby Congress to install extreme medical privacy laws, many of us with treatable diseases and conditions that might have been discovered by the dissemination of medical data would suffer or die unnecessarily.

The Privacy Debate Highlights the Need for Tolerance

If I am correct, terrorists and criminals have found unwitting allies in a large number of Americans who are so worried about the possible exposure of their minor vices or medical conditions that they support a privacy regime which would weaken the ability of government to combat terror and crime. This is actually nothing new. During Prohibition, mainstream Americans who liked a drink now and then were the de facto allies of gangsters. In the case of Prohibition, the tension between the ideal of abstinence from alcohol and the practice of widespread drinking was resolved in favor of the practice. Perhaps a similar approach is needed for many of the behaviors that Americans feel obliged to conceal.

Much of the resistance to biometric cameras might be eliminated if minor vices were legalized, or if prosecutors made it clear that victimless (and propertyless) crimes caught on camera would rarely be prosecuted. Ditto extending the kind of social tolerance already shown toward premarital sex to the use of personal ads, potency-enhancing drugs, cosmetic surgery, and the consumption of pornography—all practices that remain taboo.

At present the dinner conversation of the chattering classes tends to revolve around abs and low-carb diets. The boundaries of crassness would not be pushed much further if someone casually said, "This is Mary, whom I met in the Bondage and Submission chat room." (We already suspect that many of the couples we know did not meet in the circumstances they describe.)

One of the slogans of the '60s was, "The issue is not the issue." In many of today's heated arguments about privacy, the issue is not the issue either. The privacy debate is being driven by something nobody discusses: changing conceptions of shame in our society. Until we recognize this, it will continue to be a surrogate for another, and perhaps more important, debate.

Stronger Privacy Protection Laws Are Unnecessary

by Amitai Etzioni

About the author: *Amitai Etzioni is the author of* The Limits of Privacy *and teaches at George Washington University.*

[As of September 2001] members of Congress are returning to Capitol Hill, having assessed what's on voters' minds. They may have found that privacy ranks much lower among the public's concerns than the chattering classes report. And for good reasons.

Commentators have kept up a drumbeat about ever-rising threats to privacy. In Tampa, Florida, the police are reported to feed mug shots of crime suspects into computers connected to cameras that scan the faces of people in the street. Dick Armey, House majority leader, railed against cameras introduced to catch red-light runners. New police flashlights measure the alcohol on one's breath. New software from Microsoft and AOL is said to pose new threats to privacy.

Little wonder one of the new cliches is that privacy is at the same spot on the public learning—and alarm—curve as the environment was in the 1960s. And there are plenty of volunteers to don the Rachel Carson [a pioneer of environmentalist advocacy] mantle and do for privacy what she did for nature in her book "Silent Spring." At least half a dozen books bemoan the death of privacy and the arrival of Big Brother. And a bunch of privacy advocacy groups keep filing legal cases against both public and private intruders.

Moreover, it is possible to find US public opinion polls that support the thesis that privacy is an endangered species. For instance, when asked if they fear loss of personal privacy by government use of the Internet and other technologies, more than half of all respondents (53 percent) said they were extremely concerned, according to a Hart-Teeter poll; another third were quite concerned. Only 1 out of 8 was not losing any sleep about such a loss.

Similarly, when asked if they wanted stronger laws to protect privacy, the majority said, in effect, "by all means." Note, however, that these are cost-free questions. It is like asking if you want more fresh air, good movies, or better government—with no additional effort or expenditure on your part. The only surprise here is that anybody demurs.

Americans' Apathy Toward Privacy Issues

But when it comes to "paying" anything for gaining more privacy, Americans reveal how strongly they really feel about alleged privacy violations. Asked if they bothered to check the privacy policy of a health or medical website they'd visited, only 1 out of 4 claimed they did. This is despite the fact that medical privacy concerns the most personal information of all. To gain a small discount, roughly 80 percent of Americans declared themselves willing and ready to divulge personal information. Asked if they would support new privacy protec-

> *"The simple fact is that we have more laws and regulations to protect privacy than we had ... since the right to privacy became part of the Constitution."*

tions if they hindered investigative journalism, the public clamor for more privacy quieted down substantially. John Schwartz just reported in the *New York Times* that companies that sell privacy-protecting software have a hard time finding a market.

In addition, when Americans are asked to rank privacy among other things they care about, in numerous polls they do not rank it particularly high. Reforming Medicare and introducing gun control typically rank higher.

The leading privacy researcher, Alan Westin, reviewed numerous findings and concluded that about 1 in 4 Americans is what he calls a "privacy fundamentalist"—truly agitated about it. Two-thirds of the public are what he calls "privacy pragmatics" who look at the costs and benefits involved—as they do in most other things. (The rest cannot be bothered.)

Privacy is one more area in which the public is well ahead of the crisis-mongering pundits. While President Bush nullified, deferred, opened for renegotiation, or diluted practically all of the laws and regulations President Clinton introduced in his last year in office, Mr. Bush did let stand an extensive new set of regulations that protect medical privacy.

Plenty of Privacy Protection

People may well realize that for the first time in American history, this crucial form of privacy now has full-blown federal backing, rather than depending on a wild assortment of divergent state laws. The same holds for brand new regulations protecting financial privacy and that of children age 13 and younger. The simple fact is that we have more laws and regulations to protect privacy than we had, not only since the privacy panic started, but since the right to privacy became part of the Constitution.

And while alarms are sounded daily about new technologies that intrude, the public seems to be aware that there are all kinds of new devices that protect privacy better than it ever has been protected. This may sound like the ultimate Pollyanna-ish statement until you realize, for example, that high-powered encryption is now routinely built into new computers. As a result, communications sent via e-mail are much more secure and private than those sent by snail mail (which anyone who can get to your mailbox can read) or transmitted over phone lines (easily tapped, compared with encrypted e-mail)—not to mention faxes. The same holds for storing information. Despite all the limitations of passwords, I would rather have my medical records protected by them than locked in a filing cabinet. And audit trails, routinely used by hospitals and financial institutions, allow one to determine if any unauthorized party has accessed the data—a trick no paper record could accomplish.

The proof of my thesis—that reports that privacy is dying, and that the public is worked up about it are vastly exaggerated—will come soon. Far from rushing to introduce new privacy protections, I predict, members of Congress will load their agendas with other goodies—such as more protection for the environment.

Individuals Should Not Be Allowed to Communicate Anonymously Via the Internet

by David Davenport

About the author: *David Davenport is an assistant professor in the Computer Engineering Department of Bilkent University in Ankara, Turkey.*

Anonymous communication is seen as the cornerstone of an Internet culture that promotes sharing and free speech and is overtly anti-establishment. Anonymity, so the argument goes, ensures governments cannot spy on citizens and thus guarantees privacy and free speech. The recommendations of the American Association for the Advancement of Science's conference on "Anonymous Communication Policies for the Internet" support this view. Among the findings were that "online anonymous communication is morally neutral" and that "it should be considered a strong human and constitutional right."

This view is fundamentally mistaken; by allowing anonymous communication we actually risk an incremental breakdown of the fabric of our society. The price of our freedoms is not, I believe, anonymity, but accountability. Unless individuals and, more importantly, governments can be held accountable, we lose all recourse to the law and hence risk our very freedom. The following sections argue this in more detail and suggest the only real solution is more openness, not less.

Social Justice Requires Accountability

Individuals living in a free society reap benefits in terms of sustenance, shelter, and protection. In return, they are expected to contribute to the community. Problems occur due to imbalances in this relationship. If individuals or groups acquire excessive wealth or power, or, conversely, do not receive just rewards, tension is inevitable. Small groups, such as villages or family units, where people know and depend more directly on each other, tend to be reasonably stable despite significant imbalances. However, in larger communities, such as cities or countries, such differences can quickly lead to crime, social unrest, protests, and even revolution. In circumstances where people can be largely anonymous, and the threat of punishment is thus minimal, they find it easier to justify to themselves actions against those they perceive as outsiders or enemies.

> *"Proponents of anonymous communications on the Internet . . . open the door to many forms of criminal and antisocial behavior."*

Large social groupings necessitate some sort of decision-making mechanism (monarch and government, to name two) to guide them, and a system of controls (police and judiciary) to ensure fairness and compliance. In a democratic society, citizens "consent" to such bodies resolving any problems or conflicts that may arise, rather than taking action themselves. By punishing misconduct, society aims to deter repetition of such offenses and send a clear warning to those who may be similarly tempted to violate the rights of others. The democratic system also incorporates controls (elections and laws) that ensure that governing bodies cannot abuse their position. Obviously, resolving any unfairness, whether involving individuals, groups, or the state, requires that those responsible for the problems can be held accountable. In a free and fair society, justice must exist, and be seen to exist.

Experience suggests a society relying solely on the good will and conscience of its citizens would be unlikely to succeed in ensuring justice. Similarly, attempting to guarantee justice by adopting measures preventing the very possibility of wrongdoing is unfeasible since there is little hope of covering all eventualities. We should, of course, attempt to raise individuals to be good and conscientious citizens, and take precautions in an attempt to make misbehavior impossible, but we would surely be foolish not to retain the safety net of accountability.

The Consequences of Anonymity

Accountability requires those responsible for any misconduct be identified and brought to justice. However, if people remain anonymous, by definition, they cannot be identified, making it impossible to hold them accountable. Proponents of anonymous communications on the Internet thus open the door to many forms of criminal and antisocial behavior, while leaving victims and society helpless. Internet-based crimes, such as hacking, virus writing, denial-of-service attacks, credit card fraud, harassment, and identity theft are increasing. Already, damage estimates are measured in billions of dollars per year, but the human cost, in terms of ruined reputations, loss of trust, and a general deterioration in morals, is immeasurable.

While all this is dangerous enough, there is a much more ominous aspect to anonymity. Were anonymous communication to become the default, then it would be available, not just to the private citizen, but to the state and to those individuals comprising it. Highly sensitive material could be leaked, paybacks could be made to secure lucrative deals, pressure could be placed on officials, elections could be rigged, and arrangements could be made for political opponents to be attacked or even eliminated, all with impunity. Distrusting a government accountable to the people is one thing, facilitating a government completely unaccountable is quite another. Some may argue that governments already employ anonymity to cloak clandestine operations, so it would make no difference. However, where governments do currently use it, they do so illegally. Those involved know it is wrong and know the penalties if they are caught, thus deterring all but the most desperate or naive.

Free Speech

The right to freedom of speech is a fundamental aspect of the democratic tradition. The rationale for it is simple: Ideas transform society, and any idea, no matter how bizarre it may appear initially, might ultimately prove beneficial. Citizens should thus not be unduly restricted from or punished for expressing their views, however unpalatable they may seem. The very notion of free speech under law means protecting the speaker from prosecution and persecution, thus the speaker's identity is known. While anonymous communication is not necessary for there to be free speech, it clearly ensures that no restrictions or punishments can be imposed on anyone, whatever they may say. Does this apparent benefit outweigh its costs, as advocates claim?

Freedom of speech is concerned primarily with protecting the individual against the power of the establishment, be it the political or religious authorities, or the moral majority. Anonymous communication, however, is likely to be singularly ineffective in this regard. In dictatorships and undemocratic countries where free speech is most needed, it is unlikely these regimes would make such communication available at all. Even in circumstances where anonymous communication is allowed, unless it is pervasive, its use might easily be detected and taken as an indication of wrongdoing. Besides, messages sent anonymously are unlikely to have much impact on their own. Only if the recipient of a message knows and trusts its writer is action likely to ensue.

> *"Accountability lies at the very heart of the democratic tradition and is crucial to the continued stability of a free and fair society."*

Trust is built up as a result of numerous encounters, but if the communications are truly anonymous then it is difficult to establish such a relationship. Messages sent anonymously are thus unlikely to have much impact on their own and hence reliance on anonymous communications for whistle-blowing, informing the world of human rights violations, or promulgating a political platform would seem to be misplaced.

History is made by those brave enough to speak out, despite the serious personal risks involved. Reform may take longer to come about, but surely bravery, honesty, and openness should be encouraged as a means of effecting change. Cowering behind a cloak of anonymity hardly seems an auspicious basis for profound social upheavals. Anonymity seems to offer a cheap and easy way to speak out against authority and promote change; in reality it is ineffectual and may ultimately prove to be very costly.

When it comes to more mundane personal communications, anonymity is said to have the advantage of promoting free and open exchanges, unhampered by prejudices often formed by race, gender, or religion. Text-only communications certainly remove most, though not all, such clues, but this is a transitory situation. Once voice and videoconferencing technology become widespread, few people will exchange its convenience for such nebulous gains. Of course, enabling open discussion, particularly of medical, psychological, or legal problems, is undoubtedly something valuable. It is quite natural for people to be reticent about talking openly of such personal matters, so when they need advice they either turn to professionals in such areas (who guarantee to hold client conversations in the strictest of confidence), confide in close friends (whom they trust to keep the conversation private), or turn to complete strangers (whom they hope will not learn their identity). On the Internet however, even assuming that one's identity never accidentally slipped out (to be linked with all the intimate details poured out over the months or years) and that one could trust the advice of a totally unknown confidant, anonymity can be seriously misused. There are legitimate restrictions to the right to free speech, in particular, it does not apply to libelous remarks or ones intended to defraud, or to incite hatred or violence. In order to protect the innocent, all communications must be subject to the rule of law and this, as argued here, implies that their originators must be accountable and hence not anonymous.

That communication must be subject to law should not be taken to mean the government has the right to track, intercept, or read the communication. All that is necessary is that the courts, as opposed to the government, be able to establish the source of a communication, when, and only if, it becomes the subject of legal dispute. The need for accountability requires all communication be traceable and that this information be available to courts subject to due process. It does not entail that others, even the recipient, need know the source. Authors could thus hide their identity if they wish, but on the understanding that they can still be held accountable under law.

The Way Forward

Advocates of anonymous communication claim anonymity is essential to ensure free speech on the Internet, and this outweighs any harm that might result from drug barons, the mafia, and other criminals being untouchable. I have argued that this view is mistaken. Accountability lies at the very heart of the democratic tradition and is crucial to the continued stability of a free and fair society. Removing its safety net would only encourage deceit and lead to more crime and increasing numbers of victims unable to obtain justice. More significantly, those in power could use anonymity to their own ends, making governments unaccountable. It was distrust of government that led to calls for anonymous communications as a means to ensure free speech. The end result of anonymity, however, plays right into government's hands and has little real impact in terms of free speech.

The way forward is clear: embrace accountability and reject anonymous communications. Concerned citizens can use the improved communications of the Internet to participate more fully in government. Our freedom comes at the price of vigilance. If we abdicate our responsibilities we have only ourselves to blame. Moving to a more participatory form of democratic government is a better, safer, more stable option than that offered by the quicksand of anonymity.

Accountability, openness, and honesty may sound like old-fashioned morality, but these traits have stood us in good stead. They are the price of our freedoms, a small price to pay, surely, for the right to life, liberty, and the pursuit of happiness.

Face-Recognition Technology Does Not Threaten Individual Privacy

by Solveig Singleton

About the author: *Solveig Singleton is a lawyer and senior analyst with the Competitive Enterprise Institute's Project on Technology and Innovation.*

The two dark-skinned young men, unshaven and heavily muscled, looked ominously foreign. No doubt more than one airline passenger breathed deeper in relief when security guards at the Roanoke, Virginia, airport pulled the men out of line to search their luggage and pat them down—once in the ticket line, again at the security gate and a third time before they boarded the plane. Three "random" searches to take a 20-minute flight.

Facial-recognition technology tied to a database of suspect terrorists, though, would have left the young men alone. My black-haired fiance and his brother are no threat. Their frightening musculature is cheerfully employed shifting furniture for their mom; their closest approach to battle is the world of online computer games. Yet the human element in our security forces instinctively will bristle at their approach until the United States is attacked by blond, blue-eyed Nordic terrorists, activists for reindeer rights or some myth of Aryan superiority.

A Bad Rap

Biometrics are getting a bad rap. Fingerprinting bears the stigma of its association with police procedure. DNA databases bring to mind horrific theories of genetic or racial purity. Facial-recognition cameras call up images of George Orwell's *1984* and omnipresent video surveillance. But biometrics, like any technology, is morally neutral. Any abuses will stem from the human element in our government. And biometric systems could help to control, counter and check those error-prone human elements.

Strictly speaking, what is a biometric system? A biometric system uses personal traits or physical characteristics to recognize an individual. The signature on the back of our credit cards is a very primitive biometric; so is any photo ID or mug shot. The human optic nerve is hooked to our own brain's biological facial-recognition database. Bloodhounds track trails of unique individual scents.

Examples of more-advanced biometric systems in use include a facial-recognition system used by the West Virginia Department of Motor Vehicles to scan applicants for duplicate or fraudulent driver's licenses. The state of Georgia now includes a digital thumbprint on its licenses. Typing and mouse-use patterns also can be used to identify individuals, existing technology likely to be deployed online. Predictive Networks, a Cambridge, Massachusetts, company, has developed software to do just that. High-tech spy thrillers on television and in the movies have acquainted us with the retinal scans, voice prints and hand-geometry scanners just beginning to be deployed. The gambling industry is considering the use of voice-recognition technology to control access to telephone gambling networks, for example. Less-familiar biometric systems include earlobe analysis and body-odor sniffers. But

> *"Biometrics are getting a bad rap."*

widespread deployment of biometric systems still is part of a sci-fi future.

In that future, the trends suggest that biometrics will be a boon to privacy and security in the private sector. In the works is voice-print technology that will recognize only authorized users of long-distance telephone services or brokerage accounts, keeping out snoops. Handprints and iris scans can make it harder for hackers to fool computer networks, expanding the realm of possibility for authorized computer users safely to access sensitive medical records or other data remotely. Thieves of portable items such as cell phones, laptops, cars and credit cards will find their booty useless without the rightful owner's fingerprint to activate them. Most people have trouble remembering the long combinations of random letters and numbers needed for a really secure password. The digital record of one's fingerprint, though, can be scrambled into a unique personal-identification number to foil identity thieves. As the cost of this technology comes down and its accuracy is improved, widespread deployment in the private sector is almost a given wherever current identification systems lag behind security needs.

What of the use of biometrics in and by government? Some civil libertarians fear a controlled government database chock-full of biometric data and a nationwide system of scanners and controls from which there is no escape. Religious, political or racial minorities could be hunted down. Rogue police could harass innocents that unwittingly have offended them.

A New System Is Needed

Will biometrics facilitate human-rights violations on a trivial or massive scale? The short answer is it could do either, but the risk is no greater than for any other modern identification technology. And it can be controlled. The choice we have is not between zero-risk and risky identification systems. It is a choice between the current systems, which do not prevent government abuses and yet are fraught with security holes and other problems, or more effective modern systems no more liable to abuse than any other.

The present reality is that the current system of identification, based on the Social Security number, signature and driver's license, has failed. In a world of open public records and long-distance financial transactions over electronic networks, the Social Security number cannot continue to function as a password. The driver's license cannot be displayed as proof of age or identity over a network. Most importantly for the evolution of systems of identification, the current system has failed to provide the degree of protection against fraud that consumers would like to have. It is proving inadequate for legitimate law-enforcement purposes as well, especially as criminals have increased mobility across jurisdictions. These legitimate purposes of law enforcement include everyday protection against ordinary criminals as well as rarer terrorist events.

One way or another, current methods of authentication must be replaced or augmented—perhaps with digital signatures, perhaps with better biometrics (the photo ID and signature already are biometrics of a weak, error-prone sort) or perhaps with some combination.

Any system of information collection is subject to abuse. Data collected by the national census can be abused, and was when data was used during World War II to relocate Japanese-Americans. Wiretapping has been abused. Even the technology built into cell phones to help authorities pinpoint the location of 911 callers could be used for nefarious purposes by an evil regime to track innocent people.

The dangers and history of government abuses are real. But at the same time they are highly speculative. Given the reality of abuses and their relative rarity in the modern U.S. context, where do we draw the line? The risk that imperfect systems of identification will provide opportunities for fraud, terrorism and other crimes also is real. And these acts, too, violate

> *"The battle to preserve civil liberties and rights is more about institutions and legal rights and powers than about this or that technology."*

our rights to security of life and limb as well as property rights. Do we know that the benefits of "leaky" systems in allowing dissidents additional leeway along with criminals will outweigh the costs? The answer probably is different at different times and places throughout history. We only can make a best guess.

Do we say, as our rule of thumb, that the government may not collect or use biometric data? That some technologies simply will be off-limits to law enforcement? This would be both unrealistic and ineffective.

Some danger of abuse, however remote, extends to any technology wielded by government. Adolf Hitler and Josef Stalin managed to create a nightmare world without any electronic biometrics at all. Human beings (neighborhood informants) also can serve as surveillance for low-tech totalitarian police, as in Communist China. Declaring certain technologies off-limits would not resolve the danger of abuse and would prevent government from effectively carrying out legitimate functions.

Holding Government Accountable

If the answer to preserving freedom is not in declaring certain technology off-limits, where does the answer lie? The battle to preserve civil liberties and rights is more about institutions and legal rights and powers than about this or that technology. The Fourth Amendment does not say that the government may not collect, keep or store information. It says the police must show probable cause and obtain a warrant from a judge to conduct a search. The police are made accountable to the judiciary. This is an institutional solution, an accountability solution, going back to the old idea of checks and balances. Other constitutional principles—the freedom of speech, protection against the confiscation of private property, the right to a jury trial and constitutional protections against torture and cruel and unusual punishments—work together to hold back the human tendencies of those who govern to take more power than we willingly would give.

Indeed, biometrics promise to make government more accountable and less likely to misuse private information. Suppose biometric technology were used to restrict the access of government employees to citizens' tax records, criminal records and other files. Logs show which government employees access the files and when. Victims of rogue employees in government offices would stand a better chance of finding who had accessed their records and holding the rogues accountable. Illicit access by hackers coming from outside the system also would be reduced.

Because biometrics can help reduce the incidence of fraud and help police track perpetrators of violence in the most high-risk zones, such as airports and nuclear facilities, it may help preserve an open society in other areas. People terrified that criminals lurk among them undetected are not people who will embrace freedom. So long as our law-enforcement networks do not meaningfully help police target and quickly identify wrongdoers, we all will have to endure more random searches, generalized surveillance and heavy regulation.

The key to preserving our liberties does not lie with declaring biometrics off-limits for governments or anyone else. It lies in the realm of ideas and beliefs, powers and rights. Authoritarianism is not a gadget, it is a state of mind.

Chapter 4

Does the Threat of Terrorism Justify Curtailment of Civil Liberties?

Chapter Preface

In the first few weeks after the September 11, 2001, terrorist attacks on America, a dominant view in America was that some restrictions on civil liberties would be necessary to help prevent future terrorist attacks. For example, law enforcement authorities might need greater freedom to search and detain suspicious individuals. In discussing the effect of these security measures on civil liberties, the metaphor of a balancing act soon emerged. For example, columnist Murray B. Light of the *Buffalo News* wrote, "The nation needs to carefully balance its security concerns with its heritage of civil rights for all."

Light issued that warning in a column advocating the preservation of civil liberties. But the theme of balance has also been taken up by those who feel that some curtailments of freedom are justified. As University of Chicago law professor Richard A. Posner argues:

> If it is true . . . that the events of September 11 have revealed the United States to be in much greater jeopardy from international terrorism than had previously been believed . . . it stands to reason that out civil liberties will be curtailed. They *should* be curtailed, to the extent that the benefits in greater security outweigh the costs in reduced liberty. All that can reasonably be asked of the responsible legislative and judicial officials is that they weigh the costs as carefully as the benefits.

Posner's views echo those of Attorney General John Ashcroft, who stated, "You can't protect the Constitution and respect it without also protecting lives." In this view, the need to protect people sometimes outweighs the benefits of preserving civil liberties.

Some pundits, however, reject the idea that civil liberties and national security are in conflict and need to be weighed against each other. For example, James X. Dempsey, deputy director for the Center for Democracy and Technology, argues:

> The debate over terrorism is being framed as a trade-off between liberty and security. But protecting civil liberties can actually promote the ability of the government to defend the common good. We guarantee the right to confront one's accusers, for example, not only as an element of human dignity but also because cross-examination exposes lies and forces the government to continue looking until the truly guilty party is found.

"Surrendering freedom does not purchase security," Dempsey concludes, "and . . . democratic values—due process, checks and balances on governmental powers, respect for dissent and diversity—are strengths, not weaknesses."

Whether civil liberties must be restricted to safeguard national security is the subject of the viewpoints in the following chapter.

Curtailment of Civil Liberties Is Justified in Times of Crisis

by Jay Winik

About the author: *Historian Jay Winik is a scholar at the University of Maryland's School of Public Affairs and the author of* April 1865: The Month That Saved America.

In 1995, a little-known operative, Abdul Hakim Murad, was arrested in the Philippines on a policeman's hunch. Inside Murad's apartment were passports and a homemade bomb factory—beakers, filters, fuses and funnels; gallons of sulfuric acid and nitric acid; large cooking kettles.

Handed over to intelligence agents, Murad was violently tortured. For weeks, according to the book "Under the Crescent Moon," agents struck him with a chair and pounded him with a heavy piece of wood, breaking nearly every rib. But Murad said nothing. He taunted them. So they forced water into his mouth. They crushed lighted cigarettes into his private parts. Even then, he remained silent.

In the end, they broke him through a psychological trick. A few Philippine agents posed as members of Israel's Mossad and told Murad they were taking him to Israel. Terrified of being turned over to the Israelis, he finally told all. Then and only then.

And what a treasure trove of information it was. One of his roommates was Ramzi Yousef, a mastermind of the 1993 World Trade Center bombing, now serving a 240-year term in a U.S. prison. More ominously, Murad recounted a horrific plot to assassinate Pope John Paul II in Manila, simultaneously blow up 11 U.S. airplanes in the Pacific, and fly another plane, loaded with nerve gas, into the Central Intelligence Agency.

One wonders, of course, what would have happened if Murad had been in American custody?

It is no idle question. Today our international might may be at its zenith, but we as a nation have never been more vulnerable to debilitating and destabilizing attacks at home. As the U.S. ponders a largely hidden enemy, potentially armed with bioweapons—anthrax, plague, even smallpox—and perhaps a radiological bomb, one of the most important decisions the nation faces is how we balance the security measures we need to forestall future attacks with America's much-cherished doctrine of civil liberties.

Civil Liberties Have Survived Previous Crises

It is commonly agreed that our greatest breakthroughs in this war will most likely come not from military strikes or careful diplomacy—needed and important as they both are—but from crucial pieces of information: a lead about a terrorist cell; a confession from a captured bin Laden associate; reliable intercepts warning that a new attack is going to take place. Indeed, one small lead could potentially save thousands or hundreds of thousands of lives—perhaps millions.

But how we go about obtaining this information also raises crucial questions: When is detention going too far? When is the surveillance too much? Is e-mail fair game? Or is wartime censorship acceptable? (Already the administration has asked the media not to air the recent Osama bin Laden tapes, as well as to edit his transcripts.) And at what point are we giving government more power than is necessary, as well as unbridled access to personal information, thereby jeopardizing or perverting our precious democratic institutions?

But if history is any guide—and it is—we see that the Bush administration's proposals, even at the far end of the ledger, pale in comparison to what previous wartime administrations have imposed. Ironically, we may be the first generation of Americans to wrestle so intensely with this issue. Faced with the choice between security and civil liberties in times of crisis, previous presidents—John Adams, Abraham Lincoln, Woodrow Wilson and

> *"The Bush administration's proposals, even at the far end of the ledger, pale in comparison to what previous wartime administrations have imposed."*

Franklin Roosevelt—to a man (and with little hesitation) chose to drastically curtail civil liberties. It is also worth noting that despite these previous and numerous extreme measures, there was little long-term or corrosive effect on society after the security threat had subsided. When the crisis ended, normalcy returned, and so too did civil liberties, invariably stronger than before.

During John Adams's administration in 1798–99, war hysteria over a looming conflict with France (many feared a French invasion) gripped the young American republic. French refugees, once welcomed, were viewed as potential spies. Singers of the "Marseillaise" were hissed off Philadelphia stages. And Congress passed the Alien and Sedition Acts, considered one of the lowest points in U.S. history.

The acts provided the government with sweeping powers to deport any alien considered dangerous to the nation's welfare, as well as to impose fines and heavy imprisonment on anyone found guilty of writing, publishing, uttering or printing anything of "a false, scandalous and malicious" nature against the government. Thomas Jefferson privately called it "the reign of witches" and many Republicans openly worried that the Federalist administration was abandoning the principles of the Enlightenment, the Revolution and the Constitution. (In one telling instance, a congressman, thrown in jail for four months, was re-elected while serving his sentence.)

> *"Wartime restrictions on civil liberties have neither been irrevocable nor have they curtailed our fundamental freedoms in times of peace."*

Yet if Adams's administration was harsh, Abraham Lincoln's during the Civil War was considerably harsher. The president suspended the writ of habeas corpus and subjected "all persons discouraging volunteer enlistments" to martial law. To enforce this decree, a network of provost marshals promptly imprisoned several hundred antiwar activists and draft resisters, including five newspaper editors, three judges, a number of doctors, lawyers, journalists and prominent civic leaders.

Opposition to Lincoln's war aims was considered opposition to the war itself, and scores of opponents, including well-known citizens, respected police commissioners and even a police chief, were subject to military arrest. One estimate is that throughout the war Lincoln detained 13,535 people. Many were held for extended periods, though the government never offered any evidence against them or brought the prisoners to trial. Quite a few were guilty of little more than southern sympathies or lukewarm Unionism. When Chief Justice Roger B. Taney declared Lincoln's suspension of habeas corpus unconstitutional, Lincoln flatly refused to obey the ruling.

At one point, Union troops even sealed off Frederick, Md., and arrested 31 state legislators to prevent them from voting for the state to secede. At another point, Ulysses Grant issued his infamous "Jew Order," expelling all Jews from the region under his command (a storm of pressure forced him to rescind the order). Even congressmen were not safe. In the middle of the night, one of Lincoln's generals arrested Rep. Clement Vallandigham of Ohio and threw him in jail. Vallandigham's offense: "disloyal sentiments and speeches." When cries of despotism by his political opposition mounted, Lincoln commuted Vallandigham's sentence from imprisonment to . . . banishment; he was forcibly escorted by the military out of the Union.

Restrictions on Civil Liberties During the World Wars

Even a change of century did little to protect civil liberties in time of war. A week after World War I was declared, Woodrow Wilson created the Committee on Public Information to mobilize public opinion. Designed to help sell war bonds, combat absenteeism in the factories, and reconcile doubters to the war, this propaganda committee also cultivated a kind of war madness. All dissent became suspect: There were continual spy scares, witch hunts and even kangaroo courts that imposed harsh sentences of actual tar and feathering. The Espionage Act of 1917 followed, giving the postmaster general the authority to prevent publications from using the U.S. mail, while the subsequent Trading with the Enemy Act provided sweeping authority to censor the foreign-language press.

Then, in 1918, the newly passed Sabotage and Sedition Acts went even further, empowering the federal government to punish any expression of opinion considered "disloyal, profane, scurrilous or abusive." Activist Eugene V. Debs was imprisoned for a decade after expressing antiwar views. People were regularly hauled into court for as little as criticizing the Red Cross or questioning war financing, and the mail was summarily closed to publications that espoused socialism or feminism or displayed an anti-British bias.

World War II produced a whole new set of draconian curbs on civil liberties. After Japan's attack on Pearl Harbor, Franklin Roosevelt personally signed the infamous Executive Order 9066, authorizing the expulsion of "all persons" of Japanese ancestry (70% of whom were U.S. citizens), from their West Coast homes. Forced to leave on a week's notice, more than 110,000 were shipped by bus and train to "relocation centers," where they were herded into primitive camps rimmed by barbed wire and patrolled by armed guards. None had been accused of any crime. Nor had there been any instances of sabotage or spying. (FDR's intelligence services, for the most part, determined that few posed a risk; in fact, a number of the detainees had husbands, sons and fathers serving in the U.S. armed forces.)

Nevertheless, they were incarcerated until 1946—months after the war with Japan ended. By then, some 80% of the internees' property had been damaged by looting and vandalism; when the camps finally closed, many had lost everything. Ironically, however unconstitutional many of FDR's policies may seem to us today, they were not even controversial until a generation later.

Democracy Can Survive Temporary Restrictions

It is hard to think of a group of presidents more passionate in their staunch support of democracy than Adams, Lincoln, Wilson and Roosevelt. Yet they— Federalists, Republicans and Democrats alike—did not hesitate to enact harsh, even ruthless measures in times of national crisis. And however shocking, flawed or atrocious their actions may appear in hindsight, it is crucial to note that each president (save perhaps Lincoln) did so when there was, ultimately, no overwhelming "fire in the rear," no credible widespread, subversive threat within our own borders. Today, however, we may be facing just such a threat, and one that is largely without historical parallel.

To respond, we as a nation will have to confront some hard choices. The enormity of the risk to civilian lives on American soil is unprecedented, yet despite this the Bush administration has thus far shown remarkable restraint. But as the president weighs what additional measures will be needed, both the administration and civil libertarians would do well to recall that our history demonstrates that wartime restrictions on civil liberties have neither been irrevocable nor have they curtailed our fundamental freedoms in times of peace. Indeed, our democracy can, and has, outlived temporary restrictions and continued to thrive.

And if, as we get thicker into this grim conflict, the administration deems it necessary to enact more restrictive steps, we need not fear. When our nation is again secure, so too will be our principles.

The Use of Military Tribunals to Try Suspected Terrorists Is Justified

by Bruce Tucker Smith

About the author: *Bruce Tucker Smith is a U.S. administrative-law judge and serves as a reservist in the Air Force Judge Advocate General's Department.*

The United States is at war and, in these extraordinary times, the law must be wielded not as a shield but as a sword. The legal response to the terrorist attacks must be an integral part of, not distinct from, America's war effort. Tribunals will be swift, certain and fair. They will provide basic due process and will vindicate an aggrieved nation. Above all, the tribunals will render justice quickly: Justice delayed is most assuredly justice denied.

Unaccustomed as we are to hearing a president speak as a wartime commander in chief, ours has done so, declaring that a national emergency warrants activation of military tribunals to hear the prosecutions of those persons who wrought our latest day of infamy. Those noncitizen terror warriors who will stand before the tribunals are not entitled to the full protections of a system they most certainly would have destroyed.

The Dual Nature of Terrorism

The United States assuredly is at war in the factual sense but not precisely in the legal sense. That uncertainty poses a dilemma: What to do with a terror warrior once he is run to ground, for he is neither a lawful combatant nor a criminal in the classic sense. Military tribunals seem a highly appropriate forum in which to resolve the interwoven legal, factual and political issues raised in this new war by and against terrorism.

Legally speaking, the definition of terrorism lies somewhere in the murky half-light between war and crime. Either appellation fits, but neither suits. Admittedly, this is not a congressionally declared war between "states," because neither al-Qaeda nor the Taliban is a recognizable "state." They neither govern, at least in the classic sense, a defined territory nor engage in formal international relations with other "states." Thus, it might be overreaching to call their actions "war crimes."

Conversely the heinous acts of September 11 (together with prior, related, attacks on the USS *Cole*, Khobar Towers, etc.) are more than a series of ordinary criminal actions by independent actors. There is certainly an odor of highly coordinated state sponsorship behind the villainy.

The unclear legal nature of this new war dictates that neither domestic criminal courts, military courts-martial nor international courts are appropriate prosecutorial venues.

> *"Military tribunals . . . will ensure that the dictates of both fundamental fairness and national security are quickly met."*

Trials in civilian criminal courts would marginalize the importance of those prosecutions. The September 11 attacks transcend common criminality because terrorism of this magnitude is a political statement and an assault against American society itself. When terrorists targeted U.S. citizens on such a massive scale, they violated even the legitimate acts of war under international law.

Sadly, in the last decade we failed to recognize terror warriors for what they were. We regarded them as ordinary criminals and afforded them all the constitutional protections our criminal-justice system provides. Witness the two federal prosecutions resulting from the 1993 World Trade Center bombing. The first trial lasted more than five months, suffered a parade of more than 200 witnesses and endured the presentation of more than a thousand exhibits. The second trial was nearly eight months long and saw as many witnesses and nearly as much evidence. Of greater importance, a message was lost on the nation at large: Had the United States prosecuted those terrorists before military tribunals, Americans might have been awakened to a pre-existing and ongoing state of war that finally was brought into specific relief on September 11.

The Best Solution

Civilian courts insist upon unanimity among 12 jurors to sustain a criminal conviction. That tradition is rooted in the premise that we would rather free the guilty than condemn the innocent. But when the very real probability exists that terrorists (who are not U.S. citizens and who may be in this country illegally) likely will inflict mass murder and property damage anew, the niceties of traditional due process become untenable. The scale of the terrorist attacks has been too great; the perspective of civilian courts too narrow. The probability of time-consuming "loopholery" and attorney grandstanding are certain; the promise of a media-driven spectacle is a given. Open-air civilian courts simply are the wrong place to prosecute terror warriors.

Trial by military courts-martial is equally inappropriate because, generally speaking, military courts-martial provide more procedural due process to the accused than do most civilian courts and certainly far more than terrorists deserve. The people of the United States certainly will ask why the United States would afford the same legal protections to terrorists as it guarantees those U.S. servicemembers who defend the nation.

A third option, trial before an international court (such as those hearing Serbian and Rwandan war-crimes prosecutions), is inappropriate because the United States would have virtually no control over either the proceedings or the punishments. The greatest risk, of course, is that other national political agendas would work their way into the spotlight, and any given trial could turn into a referendum on U.S. foreign policy.

The best solution, trials before military tribunals, will ensure that the dictates of both fundamental fairness and national security are quickly met.

Criticisms of Military Tribunals

There is nothing legally inappropriate nor historically inconsistent about the reactivated tribunals. Presidents Abraham Lincoln and Franklin D. Roosevelt made extensive use of tribunals during the Civil War and World War II, respectively, and the Supreme Court has twice affirmed the constitutionality of the tribunals. In *Ex Parte Quirin*, 317 U.S. 1 (1942), the court noted, "The . . . enemy combatants who without uniform come secretly through the lines for the purpose of waging war by destruction of life or property, are . . . offenders against the law of war subject to trial and punishment by military Tribunals." And, in *Re: Yamashita*, 327 U.S. 1 (1946), the court said military tribunals are not bound by the dictates of due process as we are in our everyday civilian courts. It is noteworthy, however, that tribunals employed during World War II acquitted some German and Japanese defendants.

Criticism that the tribunals do not afford potential defendants enough procedural protection is ironic for, in reality, terrorists are entitled to no due-process rights whatsoever. International law says that only "lawful" enemy combatants are entitled to due process, established by proof that those combatants fight under a clearly designated flag or symbol visible at a distance; serve in a military force under a recognized chain of command; carry arms openly to establish combatant status clearly; and engage in operations in accord with the established laws of war.

> *"Tribunals will dispense justice swiftly and fairly, without unnecessary pretrial proceedings or lengthy post-trial appeals."*

It is doubtful that the al-Qaeda terrorists qualify as lawful combatants. Hence, the procedural rights identified in the president's order—or any procedures at present being crafted by attorneys for the departments of Defense and Justice—

are far more than the al-Qaeda terror warriors legally are entitled to receive.

It was never thinkable that even terrorists would be denied fair process. That is why the commander in chief's order specifically affirms due process and carefully directs that only noncitizens will stand before the tribunals. The order does not contemplate the prosecution of U.S. citizens or even enemy soldiers who obey the laws of armed conflict. Anyone arrested, detained or tried in the United States by a tribunal will be able to challenge the tribunal's jurisdiction through a writ of habeas corpus in an appropriate federal court. Moreover, tribunal hearings will be "full and fair." Every person tried before a tribunal will be informed of the charges against him, be represented by qualified counsel and be allowed to present a defense. The order also ensures judicial review by civilian courts.

Tribunals will not be trials by traditional military courts-martial; the rules will be entirely different. Yet, the subtext of the criticism leveled against the tribunals is that a defendant cannot get a fair trial; that somehow, a trial by military judges and prosecutors would be a sham. Such criticism is utterly without merit and horribly uninformed. Tribunals will be designed, prosecuted, defended and adjudicated by the best attorneys in uniform—counselors at law who have been educated at U.S. law schools and who have been steeped in a tradition of respect for the due-process rights of the accused.

During my nearly two decades of service as both a military prosecutor and defense counsel, it has been demonstrated repeatedly to me that those men and women practicing within our U.S. military-justice system simply are the finest such practitioners in the world. Unlike their civilian counterparts, military lawyers are governed by appellate case law, which actually forbids unlawful political or command influence over proceedings, ensures vigorous defense advocacy by competent counsel and insists upon procedural fairness. This is the rich cultural and legal soil from which the participants in the tribunals have grown.

Swift and Effective

Tribunals are the best solution because civilian jurors and judges won't have to face personal risks that may be attendant to terrorist trials. Tribunals allow the government to use classified information as evidence without compromising either national security or the lives of Americans on the front lines of battle. Tribunals will dispense justice swiftly and fairly, without unnecessary pretrial proceedings or lengthy post-trial appeals, lest other terrorists become emboldened by the slow grind of our criminal-justice system.

Whether trying terrorists by tribunal will lower the United States in the esteem of the world community is utterly irrelevant. Those who have admired the United States will continue to do so; those who revile us will not change their minds simply because we offered the full panoply of procedural due process to terrorists.

Chapter 4

Our focus must remain constant and vigilant: We are at war and we must free ourselves of the notion that the September 11 terror attacks merely were crimes to be resolved in our often tediously slow criminal courts. We must appreciate that the tribunals are a necessary part of the war effort.

The tribunals are a sword that must be wielded with speed, but most certainly with due care.

The Use of Torture May Be Justified in Certain Circumstances

by Alan M. Dershowitz

About the author: *Alan M. Dershowitz is a Harvard law professor and the author of* Shouting Fire: Civil Liberties in a Turbulent Age.

The FBI's frustration over its inability to get material witnesses to talk has raised a disturbing question rarely debated in this country: When, if ever, is it justified to resort to unconventional techniques such as truth serum, moderate physical pressure and outright torture?

The constitutional answer to this question may surprise people who are not familiar with the current U.S. Supreme Court interpretation of the 5th Amendment privilege against self-incrimination: Any interrogation technique, including the use of truth serum or even torture, is not prohibited. All that is prohibited is the introduction into evidence of the fruits of such techniques in a criminal trial against the person on whom the techniques were used. But the evidence could be used against that suspect in a non-criminal case—such as a deportation hearing—or against someone else.

If a suspect is given "use immunity"—a judicial decree announcing in advance that nothing the defendant says (or its fruits) can be used against him in a criminal case—he can be compelled to answer all proper questions. The issue then becomes what sorts of pressures can constitutionally be used to implement that compulsion.

We know that he can be imprisoned until he talks. But what if imprisonment is insufficient to compel him to do what he has a legal obligation to do? Can other techniques of compulsion be attempted?

Let's start with truth serum. What right would be violated if an immunized suspect who refused to comply with his legal obligation to answer questions truthfully were compelled to submit to an injection that made him do so?

Excerpted from "Is There a Torturous Road to Justice?" by Alan M. Dershowitz, *Los Angeles Times*, November 8, 2001. Copyright © 2001 by the Times Mirror Company. Reprinted with permission.

Not his privilege against self-incrimination, since he has no such privilege now that he has been given immunity.

What about his right of bodily integrity? The involuntariness of the injection itself does not pose a constitutional barrier. No less a civil libertarian than Justice William J. Brennan rendered a decision that permitted an allegedly drunken driver to be involuntarily injected to remove blood for alcohol testing. Certainly there can be no constitutional distinction between an injection that removes a liquid and one that injects a liquid.

What about the nature of the substance injected? If it is relatively benign and creates no significant health risk, the only issue would be that it compels the recipient to do something he doesn't want to do. But he has a legal obligation to do precisely what the serum compels him to do: answer all questions truthfully.

Torture Warrants?

What if the truth serum doesn't work? Could the judge issue a "torture warrant," authorizing the FBI to employ specified forms of non-lethal physical pressure to compel the immunized suspect to talk?

Here we run into another provision of the Constitution—the due process clause, which may include a general "shock the conscience" test. And torture in general certainly shocks the conscience of most civilized nations.

But what if it were limited to the rare "ticking bomb" case—the situation in which a captured terrorist who knows of an imminent large-scale threat refuses to disclose it?

Would torturing one guilty terrorist to prevent the deaths of a thousand innocent civilians shock the conscience of all decent people?

To prove that it would not, consider a situation in which a kidnapped child had been buried in a box with two hours of oxygen. The kidnapper refuses to disclose its location. Should we not consider torture in that situation?

All of that said, the argument for allowing torture as an approved technique, even in a narrowly specified range of cases, is very troubling.

We know from experience that law enforcement personnel who are given limited authority to torture will expand its use. The cases that have generated the current debate over torture illustrate this problem. And, concerning the arrests made following the September 11 attacks, there is no reason to believe that the detainees know about specific future terrorist targets. Yet there have been calls to torture these detainees.

> *"Would torturing one guilty terrorist to prevent the deaths of thousands of innocent civilians shock the conscience of all decent people?"*

I have no doubt that if an actual ticking bomb situation were to arise, our law enforcement authorities would torture. The real debate is whether such torture should take place outside of our legal system or within it. The answer to this seems clear: If we are to have torture, it should be authorized by the law.

Judges should have to issue a "torture warrant" in each case. Thus we would not be winking an eye of quiet approval at torture while publicly condemning it.

Democracy requires accountability and transparency, especially when extraordinary steps are taken. Most important, it requires compliance with the rule of law. And such compliance is impossible when an extraordinary technique, such as torture, operates outside of the law.

Government Anti-Terrorism Measures Threaten to Severely Weaken Civil Liberties

by Valerie L. Demmer

About the author: *Valerie L. Demmer is an editorial consultant at the* Humanist, *the magazine of the American Humanist Association.*

In response to the terrorist attacks of September 11, 2001, the Bush administration reacted swiftly and boldly, implementing programs it claimed would strengthen the security of the United States. President George W. Bush, Secretary of Defense Donald Rumsfeld, and Attorney General John Ashcroft have all adopted a firm and unyielding stance in executing their focused reply to the menace of global terrorism. An unfortunate byproduct of these aggressive moves, however, is the erosion of civil liberties. The administration has gone beyond the legitimate needs of national security and is infringing on constitutional freedoms in the name of patriotism and security.

The Patriot Act: Undermining the Constitution

The Patriot Act (Provide Appropriate Tools Required to Intercept and Obstruct Terrorism Act) was signed into law by Bush on October 26, 2001, after being rushed through Congress without giving members time to properly read or interpret its provisions. According to Representative Ron Paul of Texas (one of only three Republicans in the House to vote against the bill), "The bill wasn't printed before the vote—at least I couldn't get it. . . . It was a very complicated bill. Maybe a handful of staffers actually read it, but the bill definitely was not available to members before the vote."

In an interview given to *Insight,* Paul further said, "The insult is to call this a 'patriot bill' and suggest I'm not patriotic because I insisted upon finding out what is in it and voting no. I thought it was undermining the Constitution, so I didn't vote for it—and therefore I'm somehow not a patriot. That's insulting."

Ostensibly an anti-terrorist bill, the Patriot Act makes changes to over fifteen different statutes. Of particular concern, the legislation permits the government to arbitrarily detain or deport suspects; to eavesdrop on Internet communications, monitor financial transactions, and obtain individuals' electronic records; and to clandestinely survey records of religious and political organizations, whose privacy rights have usually been upheld in the courts. Critics of the act contend that these McCarthy-like tactics strip citizens of their fundamental rights while not being effective in—and often not having anything to do with—stopping terrorism.

> *"Of course there is no doubt that, if we lived in a police state, it would be easier to catch terrorists."*

The act even allows increased surveillance of church finances and bookstore records. For example, instead of being able to ask a court to quash a subpoena for customer information, booksellers may be required to turn records over immediately. The act allows surveillance through all types of electronic communications and affects telecommunications companies, Internet providers, cable companies—indeed anyone using this technology. Jim Dempsey, deputy director of the Center for Democracy and Technology, worries that investigators "will collect more information on innocent people and be distracted from the task of actually identifying those who may be planning future attacks."

Russ Feingold (Democrat-Wisconsin), the only dissenting voice in the Senate, addressed his colleagues in the Senate before the bill's passage, pointing out that the framers of the U.S. Constitution, even though they'd just been through a war with Britain, "wrote a Constitution of limited powers and an explicit Bill of Rights to protect liberty in times of war, as well as in times of peace." Feingold added:

> Of course there is no doubt that, if we lived in a police state, it would be easier to catch terrorists. If we lived in a country that allowed the police to search your home at any time for any reason; if we lived in a country that allowed the government to open your mail, eavesdrop on your phone conversations, or intercept your email communications; if we lived in a country that allowed the government to hold people in jail indefinitely based on what they write or think, or based on mere suspicion that they are up to no good, then the government would no doubt discover and arrest more terrorists.
>
> But that probably would not be a country in which we would want to live. And that would not be a country for which we could, in good conscience, ask our young people to fight and die. In short, that would not be America.
>
> Preserving our freedom is one of the main reasons that we are now engaged in this new war on terrorism. We will lose that war without firing a shot if we sacrifice the liberties of the American people.

Sacrificing Liberties

And sacrificing liberties is just what the Bush administration would do. It announced last fall that 5,000 men between the ages of eighteen and thirty-three were being rounded up by the FBI for questioning. The young men have been in the country for two years and are from "suspect" countries. The list was provided by Ashcroft, who emphasized that "the objective is to collect any information that the individuals on this list may have regarding terrorist elements in this country and abroad. These individuals were selected for interviews because they fit the criteria of persons who might have knowledge of foreign-based terrorists." This action was denounced by the Center for Constitutional Rights in a press release which stated: "Questioning individuals without any evidence of wrongdoing amounts to the very definitions of racial profiling. . . . Since September 11, we have already seen thousands of people who have been harassed by local authorities over immigration matters totally unrelated to the attacks."

In another disturbing development, Ashcroft approved a rule that permits eavesdropping by the Justice Department on the confidential conversations of inmates and uncharged detainees with their lawyers—communication that is supposed to be inviolate. Robert Hirshon, president of the American Bar Association stated: "Prior judicial approval and the establishment of probable cause . . . are required if the government's surveillance is to be consistent with the Constitution and is to avoid abrogating the rights of innocent people." Ashcroft's rule, however, was pushed through as an emergency measure without a waiting period. Senator Patrick J. Leahy (Democrat-Vermont), in a letter to Congress said, "I am deeply troubled at what appears to be an executive effort to exercise new powers without judicial scrutiny or statutory authorization."

> *"We should never be so fearful as to think somehow we can gain a great measure of security by being willing to set aside the Bill of Rights."*

Indeed, unilateral executive action is becoming a trend of this administration. For instance, on November 13, [2001,] Bush issued a military order directing Rumsfeld to be responsible for military tribunals to try noncitizens charged with terrorism. Secret trials without benefit of a jury or the requirement of a unanimous verdict, as well as nondisclosure of evidence for "national security reasons," would be authorized by the use of these tribunals. Representative John Conyers (Democrat-Michigan, and the ranking member of the House Judiciary Committee) called Bush's order "a civil liberties calamity in this country" that puts the "executive branch in the unattainable role of legislator, prosecutor, judge and jury." At a press conference, Conyers, other Democratic legislators, and Representative Bob Barr (Republican-Georgia) described the military tribunals as an abuse of executive power jeopardizing the nation's civil liberties. Immediate hearings were called for by Barr. Representative Dennis Kucinich (Democrat-

Ohio) said, "We should never be so fearful as to think somehow we can gain a great measure of security by being willing to set aside the Bill of Rights or any other hallowed legal principle that forms the bedrock of our society."

On December 6, Ashcroft appeared before the Senate Judiciary Committee for a lengthy hearing on Bush's order to use military tribunals, the Justice Department's monitoring of phone conversations between suspects and their lawyers, and the questioning of thousands of people of Middle Eastern heritage. Ashcroft was defiant, denied these actions undermine civil liberties, and charged that accusations promoting fear of lost freedom aid terrorists. The next day, the American Humanist Association commented, "Our nation is built on diversity, not unanimity, and is not bolstered by governmental attempts to suppress dissent. We appeal to Congress and the president to halt Ashcroft's assault on America's civil liberties."

Unfortunately, the current crackdown on civil liberties is nothing new, and the Bush administration is using earlier infringements on freedoms to justify its new policies. In World War I there was press censorship. During World War II, Japanese-Americans and other foreign-born citizens were interned. The Cold War era had its McCarthyism with blacklisting of suspected communist sympathizers. During the Vietnam War, anti-war protest groups were infiltrated, harassed, and spied on. The Gulf War saw media coverage controlled through "pool reporting." As Feingold put it: "Wartime has sometimes brought us the greatest tests of our Bill of Rights."

In the first days and weeks immediately following the September 11 tragedies, a wave of nationalism swept across the United States the likes of which hadn't been seen since World War II. But with this wave of patriotism came a zeal threatening the very ideals the United States stands for.

Attacks on Freedom of Expression

In particular, the right to freedom of expression has been compromised. In one incident, the cartoon Boondocks was pulled from some newspapers in New York because it was deemed either "un-American" or too political. Rick Stromoski, cartoonist of Soup to Nutz and spokesperson for the National Cartoonists Society said, "I find that a little scary, that just because someone can take another point of view they're seen as unpatriotic or sympathetic to the terrorists. . . . Papers are afraid of offending their communities and losing even more readers."

The same could be said about television programs. Bill Maher's *Politically Incorrect* was dropped by fifteen stations after remarks he made after September 11 were deemed inappropriate. . . .

Airport security has understandably been a prime concern since the terrorist attacks. But in the name of "national security" some passengers' civil liberties have been violated. Green Party USA coordinator Nancy Oden was stopped by government agents while trying to board an American Airlines flight in Bangor, Maine, in October. She wasn't arrested for anything—merely prevented from flying. Oden had been scheduled to speak at the Greens' national committee meeting in Chicago to work on details of a campaign against biochemical warfare and the party's peace agenda. According to Oden, "An official told me that my name had been flagged in the computer. . . . I was targeted because the Green Party USA opposes the bombing of innocent civilians in Afghanistan." Chicago Green activist Lionel Trepanier commented, "The attack on the right of association of an opposition political party is chilling. The harassment of peace activists is reprehensible."

On November 1 Circuit Court Judge James Stucky upheld the three-day suspension handed down by Sissonville High School officials against Charleston, West Virginia, student Katie Sierra for promoting an "Anarchy Club" and wearing anti-war T-shirts in school. In October, high-school student Aaron Pettit of Fairview Park, Ohio, was suspended for ten days for displaying anti-war posters on his locker—one depicting an eagle with a tear drop and others with bombers drawn on them with messages like "May God have mercy, because we will not." Pettit sued the school in federal court and was reinstated. Even teachers have been suspended for merely voicing their views about the military action and policies now enacted.

> *"In the name of 'national security' some [airline] passengers' civil liberties have been violated."*

Websites have also been shut down. Hypervine, an Internet service provider, forced Cosmic Entertainment to pull three radio show sites on the Internet, among them Al Lewis Live, because they allegedly contained pro-terrorist materials. The sites were reportedly forced from the Net when Hypervine received calls from someone identifying himself as a federal agent and threatening seizure of Hypervine's assets if the sites weren't shut down. Al Lewis, who played Grandpa in the 1960s television show *The Munsters*, said, "I lived through the McCarthy period. It will get worse."

Apparently intimidated by developments immediately following the terrorist attacks, the Sierra Club and the Natural Resources Defense Council began voluntarily removing ad material that criticized Bush's environmental policies. The Sierra Club went so far as to remove material critical of Bush prior to September 11.

An October 4 article by Brook Shelby Biggs, contributing editor of MotherJones.com aptly sums up the clamp down on civil liberties:

> Far more surprising than government attempts to stifle criticism is the seeming willingness of the media, politicians, and activist groups—particularly those on the left—to censor themselves. Some may be backing off to avoid the kind of public crucifixion endured by *Politically Incorrect*'s Bill Maher. Others, however, apparently truly believe that frank and vibrant discourse is damaging to the country's moral fiber.

Threats to Religious Liberty

The trauma of the terrorist attacks has caused many people to seek solace in religion—and religionists are taking advantage of it. The phrase "God Bless America" is everywhere these days. Besides the endless renditions of the song at sporting and other public events, there is a movement afoot in Congress to have the song declared a national hymn and to have the slogan "God Bless America" displayed in schools and public buildings. Moreover, a minister of the United Church of Christ has observed that the message implied by "God Bless America" is: "to be genuinely patriotic you must be conventionally religious."

Stefan Presser, legal director of the Pennsylvania American Civil Liberties Union, referring to a lawsuit that challenges the constitutionality of displaying the Ten Commandments in a public courthouse in West Chester, Pennsylvania, eloquently summarized this issue by saying, "Even if 99 out of 100 people are in favor of keeping the plaque, the point of the Bill of Rights is that the majority does not rule when it comes to religious issues. Each person, in their own privacy, gets to make religious decisions." In our zeal to protect the country from the terrorist threat let us not forget the menace posed by religious excess.

Some of these encroachments on our civil liberties—those with sunset provisions—will expire automatically unless renewed by Congress. Others will be challenged in the courts as violations of the Constitution. Still others seem destined to become permanent encroachments—what Bush and his cronies believe are "necessary accommodations" to a changing world.

We would do well to remember the words of Supreme Court Justice Oliver Wendell Holmes Jr., who said many years ago, "The life of the law has not been logic: it has been experience. The felt necessities of the time . . . have had a good deal more to do than the syllogism in determining the rules by which men should be governed."

The question we must now ask ourselves is: how do we feel about the necessities of our time? You can be sure our laws are following close behind. If you don't agree with the laws curtailing your rights and the actions of your officials, this is the time to tell your legislators and your neighbors how you feel. It's the patriotic thing to do.

The Use of Military Tribunals to Try Suspected Terrorists Is Not Justified

by the *St. Louis Post-Dispatch*

About the author: *The following viewpoint is an editorial from the* St. Louis Post-Dispatch, *a daily newspaper. It represents the opinion of the* Post-Dispatch's *editorial staff.*

President George W. Bush's plan to use military tribunals to try terrorist suspects is founded on three flawed assumptions: that military trials can be fair in the United States even if they aren't fair in other countries; that U.S. military tribunals provide the same kind of legal protections as courts-martial; and that historical precedents justify transplanting 19th century notions of fairness into the 21st century.

The claim that U.S. military tribunals will be fair is too self-serving to be credible. For years, the United States has excoriated dozens of countries—Peru, Russia, China and Sudan among others—for unfair military trials. Mr. Bush argues that our military courts will be different. That borders on a double standard.

The Right to a Fair Trial

Mr. Bush's order providing for military tribunals already has the hallmarks of unfairness: All or part of the trial could be closed. Military officers replace impartial judges and juries. Most rules of evidence are tossed out as is the requirement for proof beyond a reasonable doubt. The suspect doesn't have the right to choose a lawyer. Conviction and execution require only a two-thirds vote. Appeals to federal court are barred, effectively suspending the writ of habeas corpus.

The absence of those basic protections also refutes the White House claim that military tribunals provide terrorists with the same protections Americans receive in courts-martial. In fact, courts-martial have jury trials, appeals and unanimous verdicts. Little wonder, then, that Spain balked at turning over al-Qaida members it arrested.

Mr. Bush maintains that the tribunals could provide a safer, more efficient way of prosecuting a group of al-Qaida members captured in Afghanistan. That narrow use might not be objectionable. But Mr. Bush's order also permits the use of the tribunals to try some of the immigrants detained in the United States.

The weakest of the Bush assumptions is that history justifies the tribunals. But a careful reading of U.S. history leads to the conclusion that military tribunals should not be used when the civil courts are available.

Lincoln and Roosevelt

The White House rests its dubious defense of tribunals on World War II and the Civil War. Both episodes were dark chapters in American history, in which justice was sacrificed to presidential power. President Abraham Lincoln suspended the writ of habeas corpus—a protection against false imprisonment—during the first year of the Civil War; he ignored the chief justice who told him he could not.

In 1864, Lambdin P. Milligan, an Indiana politician, was tried before a military commission for conspiracy to release Confederate prisoners. The evidence showed that Mr. Milligan was a member of the Sons of Liberty, but little else. After the war, Justice David Davis said the president could not try Mr. Milligan or any other civilian before a military commission when the civil courts were open for business. In a famous passage—relevant today—Mr. Davis wrote: "The Constitution of the United States is a law for rulers and people, equally in war and in peace, and covers with the shield of its protection all classes of men, at all times and under all circumstances."

The most recent use of military tribunals was Franklin Roosevelt's prosecution of eight saboteurs who sneaked into the country on German submarines in 1942. One of the spies, an American citizen, tipped off the FBI, but J. Edgar Hoover boasted that he had cracked the case. Historians concluded that Mr. Roosevelt wanted a secret military trial to avoid the embarrassing revelation that Mr. Hoover had little to do with solving the crime. The seven Army major generals who heard the evidence were often confused by the law and standards of evidence. When the lawyer for the men appealed to the Supreme Court, Mr. Roosevelt's attorney general told the justices privately that the president would hang the Germans no matter what the court did. The court quickly upheld the convictions, releasing its opinion after six of the eight had been executed. That same year, the court upheld the detention of 100,000 Japanese-Americans.

> *"A careful reading of U.S. history leads to the conclusion that military tribunals should not be used when civil courts are available."*

At least Mr. Roosevelt had the approval of Congress for his tribunals. Mr. Bush does not. He insists that his war power gives him the authority to set up tribunals on his own. The Supreme Court usually defers to the president in wartime and probably would again. But when the court invalidated President Harry S Truman's seizure of the steel mills during the Korean war, it said that a president acts in a "zone of twilight" when he doesn't have Congress' acquiescence.

The U.S. goal in the upcoming prosecutions is straightforward: Bring the terrorists to justice and provide them with a trial that is both fair in reality and that looks fair in the eyes of the world.

The best road to that goal would be creating an international court, like the one at The Hague. Second best is trial in federal court. Attorney General John D. Ashcroft fears "Osama TV." Granted, big trials can be media circuses. But Mr. Ashcroft sells short our system of justice. No judge is going to permit a televised trial, O.J. Simpson–style. The most self-defeating approach is a closed military tribunal. Even if it looks fair to us, it is going to look like a kangaroo court to the rest of the world.

The Government Should Not Authorize the Use of Torture to Combat Terrorism

by Harvey A. Silverglate

About the author: *Harvey A. Silverglate is a lawyer and the coauthor of* The Shadow University: The Betrayal of Liberty on America's Campuses.

Among the unsettling effects of the September 11 terrorist attacks on New York and Washington and the anthrax mailings that followed is their triggering, seemingly overnight, of a national debate over whether the United States should practice torture—as a matter of national policy—to combat terrorism. The pro-torture camp wants to authorize law-enforcement agents to inflict intense physical pain in order to extract information from suspected terrorists (the word "suspected" is often conveniently omitted by the law's proponents) where that information might pinpoint the location of a "ticking bomb" or otherwise avert some imminent act of mass carnage.

So imagine the surprise of many long-time legal observers when Harvard Law professor Alan Dershowitz published an op-ed piece in the *Los Angeles Times* on November 8, 2001, arguing that "if we are to have torture, it should be authorized by the law" and that the authorities should be required to apply to judges for "torture warrants" in each case. A careful reading of his op-ed indicates that Dershowitz did not actually go so far as to say he favors torture. And in subsequent lectures and interviews he placed on record his personal opposition to torture. But the piece drew a firestorm of criticism from both liberals and libertarians, who argued that Dershowitz had indirectly sanctioned the use of torture and should now be regarded as a turncoat in the battle to preserve civil liberties.

Dershowitz's Argument

Nonetheless, Dershowitz's op-ed makes a fairly powerful, though flawed, argument that torture would be ruled constitutional. Under the right circumstances, he claims, torture, while "very troubling," would pass a test the Supreme Court has sometimes used to determine the constitutionality of the government's use of an extreme law-enforcement technique: whether it "shocks the conscience."

"Consider a situation in which a kidnapped child had been buried in a box with two hours of oxygen," suggests the law professor, ever the master of the difficult hypothetical. "The kidnapper refused to disclose its location," he continues. "Should we not consider torture in that situation?"

Dershowitz, clearly uncomfortable with his own rhetorical question, does not quite give a direct answer. In order to avoid an ugly answer to an impossibly difficult moral and legal question, he takes another route. Since there is "no doubt that if an actual ticking bomb situation were to arise, our law enforcement authorities would torture," he says, "the real debate is whether such torture should take place outside of our legal system or within it." The answer to this question is clear and easy for Dershowitz: "If we are to have torture, it should be authorized by law" because "democracy requires accountability and transparency."

Besides, Dershowitz argues, the Constitution poses no obstacle to legal, court-authorized, supervised torture. That's because the Fifth Amendment's protection against self-incrimination does not protect against requiring someone to testify and disclose information; it merely protects against the use of such information against the person interrogated. Thus, in the face of a court-issued "immunity" order, any citizen may be forced to testify in a judicial forum, or suffer imprisonment for the refusal to do so. Nor does Dershowitz believe that any "right of bodily integrity" that might be read into the Bill of Rights prohibits, say, the injection of "truth serum," since the Supreme Court has already authorized the forcible drawing of blood from a suspect for alcohol testing. "Certainly there can be no constitutional distinction" he argues, "between an injection that removes a liquid and one that injects a liquid." (This particular argument is spurious, and Dershowitz should know better: he is a long-time opponent of the death penalty, where the current preferred method of execution is the injection of deadly poisons into the veins of the convict.)

> *"[The Eighth Amendment] states quite plainly that no 'cruel or unusual punishments [shall be] inflicted.'"*

Dershowitz fails to mention altogether another amendment—the Eighth, which states quite plainly that no "cruel or unusual punishments [shall be] inflicted." The modern-era Supreme Court has ruled that this standard, which is inherently subjective, must be interpreted according to society's evolving standards of decency. It is likely that the pre–September 11 Court would have ruled that techniques all would agree constitute "torture" would qualify as "cruel" and (for our society, at least) "unusual." But in the atmosphere created by the ghastly attacks of September 11, the Court might now rule that it is neither cruel nor unusual to torture a convict, a prisoner, or even a mere suspect, if the information that might be wrung from that person could save thousands of innocent lives. (After all, the Supreme Court did uphold the

> *"Institutionalizing torture will give it society's imprimatur, lending it a degree of respectability."*

constitutionality of President Franklin D. Roosevelt's transfer of Japanese-Americans from the West Coast into "relocation camps" after Pearl Harbor, and of his using a military tribunal to try—and execute—German saboteurs who landed on our shores intending to destroy strategic targets.) War does change mindsets, even of the courts—and understandably so.

But leaving aside his interpretation (or neglect) of inherently vague constitutional provisions, Dershowitz's conclusion is clear: if torture is to be administered, it should require "torture warrants" issued by judges before whom the government must lay out reasons why torture—and only torture—could extract life-saving information. "Thus we would not be winking an eye of quiet approval at torture while publicly condemning it," he says.

Torture Is Wrong

Some advocates of torture justify their position on the simple ground that monsters like those who helped level the World Trade Center deserve to be tortured, ostensibly to get information that might prevent future catastrophic destruction of human life. (Of course, if the pain inflicted also goes a small way toward exacting some retribution for the WTC carnage, though the suspected terrorist had nothing to do with September 11 but is planning an entirely new attack, some would view it as a just bonus.) But Dershowitz is not in that camp. He understands that in the real world, when law-enforcement authorities have reason to believe that a suspect has information that can save lives, individual cops and agents will resort to torture no matter what. After all, we have long struggled to control the gratuitous use of torture by police on suspects from whom they seek to extract confessions, and by sadistic prison guards against inmates for no apparent practical purpose whatsoever. Can there be any real doubt that a law-enforcement officer, or, for that matter, most of us, would probably be willing to resort to the torture of a person who knew where to find our kidnapped child or where to locate an atomic bomb ticking away in some major American city?

So what, then, is wrong with a system that requires torture warrants—especially if an opponent of torture like Dershowitz can argue for their constitutionality? The answer is threefold.

186

First, institutionalizing torture will give it society's imprimatur, lending it a degree of respectability. It will then be virtually impossible to curb not only the increasing frequency with which warrants will be sought—and granted—but also the inevitable rise in *unauthorized* use of torture. Unauthorized torture will increase not only to extract life-saving information, but also to obtain confessions (many of which will then prove false). It will also be used to punish real or imagined infractions, or for no reason other than human sadism. This is a genie we should not let out of the bottle.

Second, we should think twice before entirely divorcing law from morality. There can be little doubt that until now, Americans have widely viewed torture as beyond the pale. The US rightly criticizes foreign governments that engage in the practice, and each year our Department of State issues a report that classifies foreign nations on the basis of their human-rights records, including the use of torture. Our country has signed numerous international treaties and compacts that decry the use of torture. We tamper with that hard-won social agreement at our grave moral peril.

Third, our nation sets an example for the rest of the world: we believe not only in the rule of law, but in the rule of *decent* laws, and in a government composed of decent men and women who are accountable to a long tradition. There may be more efficient ways of governing, but our system is intentionally inefficient in certain ways in order to protect liberty. Our three co-equal branches of government immediately come to mind. Also, government can almost always proceed more efficiently if it is not dogged by an independent press protected by the First Amendment. But we have found from long experience that, as Jefferson famously said, if one were forced to choose between government without the press or the press without government, the latter might well be preferable. Trials by jury are long, inefficient, expensive, and sometimes lead to the acquittal of defendants whom the state is convinced are guilty and wants very much to incarcerate or even execute. Some of those acquitted are indeed guilty. Yet trial by jury remains the best (albeit imperfect) system ever devised for ascertaining truth while curbing government excess and abuse of power. Torture may sometimes offer an efficient means of obtaining information, but efficiency should not always trump other values.

How to Handle the Extreme Cases

Yet we still face Dershowitz's "ticking bomb" hypothetical. How do we deal with that? Is it really moral, after all, to insist on having "clean hands" and to refrain from torture, when thousands or even hundreds of thousands of people could die as a result of our pious and self-righteous morality?

The answer to this quandary lies in a famous criminal-law decision rendered in Victorian England by the British appeals court known as the Queen's Bench. It is a case studied by virtually every American law student at virtually every law school. In *Regina* [the Queen] *v. Dudley and Stephens*, the court dealt with

187

one of the most difficult criminal cases in English legal history.

In July 1884, four crewmen of a wrecked English yacht were set adrift in a lifeboat more than 1,000 miles from the nearest land mass. They had no water and no food except for two one-pound tins of turnips. Three of the men—Dudley, Stephens, and Brooks—were "able-bodied English seamen," while the fourth lifeboat passenger was an 18-year-old boy who was less robust than the others and soon showed signs of weakening. As they drifted, severe hunger and thirst set in. It became clear, as the trial court found, that unless the three stronger seamen killed the boy—who by then had deteriorated substantially and was on the verge of dying anyway—and then ate his body and drank his blood, all four of them would die. "There was no appreciable chance of saving life except by killing one for the others to eat," and the boy seemed the most logical candidate since he was "likely" to die anyway, as the trial court put it. Dudley and Stephens followed this course, with Brooks dissenting. Once the boy was killed, all three partook of his flesh and blood. Four days later, the three survivors, barely alive, were rescued by a passing ship.

> **"We do not need, and should not dare to enact, a system of torture warrants in the United States."**

The Queen's Bench was faced with the question of whether, under English law, the three were guilty of murder, or whether the homicide was justified by a "defense of necessity." The judges concluded that they were guilty of murder and should be sentenced to death. "[T]he absolute divorce of law from morality would be of fatal consequence," they wrote, "and such divorce would follow if the temptation to murder in this case were to be held by law an absolute defense of it." Were this bright line against murder abandoned, warned the court, it might "be made the legal cloak for unbridled passion and atrocious crime." The genie, in other words, would have escaped from the bottle, with unimaginable consequences.

But since this case is a very hard one and the outcome—the death penalty—would strike most civilized people as excessive under the circumstances, the judges suggested a way out of the dilemma. The judges claimed that it is left "to the Sovereign"—in this instance, the Queen—"to exercise that prerogative of mercy which the Constitution has intrusted to the hands fittest to dispense it." In other words, executive clemency offers a way to trim the harsh edges of the law in the truly exceptional case.

The lesson of this case for the use of torture warrants is clear. When a law-enforcement officer truly believes that a suspect possesses life-saving information, and commits the perfectly human act of torturing the suspect to obtain that information, the officer *should* be tried for the crime of violating the suspect's constitutional rights, or for some related crime such as assault and battery or mayhem (willful bodily mutilation). If the jury, acting as the conscience of the community, decides that the officer does not deserve to be convicted and punished under the circumstances, it will acquit. Indeed, under our system of unanimous jury verdicts in federal and most state criminal trials, a single juror who refuses to vote for conviction can "hang" the jury and prevent a verdict and hence a conviction. In our legal history, there have even been instances where juries, exercising what is known as "jury nullification," have refused to convict or have acquitted obviously guilty defendants. Such verdicts are hardly unknown, as in cases of mercy killings or the medical use of marijuana.

Further, even when a conviction has been handed down in a hard case, the government's chief executive (the president of the United States or, on the state level, usually the governor) may exercise his or her constitutional authority to commute (or terminate) the sentence and free the defendant, or even pardon the defendant and thereby wipe clean his or her criminal record. In the *Dudley and Stephens* case, in fact, Queen Victoria commuted the sentence to six months' imprisonment. This is how a civilized nation upholds civic decency and the rule of law while allowing for those exceptional situations when normal human beings break the law for some greater good or under conditions of overwhelming necessity.

We do not need, and should not dare to enact, a system of torture warrants in the United States. Our legal system is perfectly capable of dealing with the exceptional hard case without enshrining the notion that it is okay to torture a fellow human being.

Organizations to Contact

The editors have compiled the following list of organizations concerned with the issues debated in this book. The descriptions are derived from materials provided by the organizations. All have publications or information available for interested readers. The list was compiled on the date of publication of the present volume; the information provided here may change. Be aware that many organizations take several weeks or longer to respond to inquiries, so allow as much time as possible.

American Civil Liberties Union (ACLU)
132 W. 43rd St., New York, NY 10036
(212) 944-9800 • fax: (212) 869-9065
e-mail: aclu@aclu.org • website: www.aclu.org

The ACLU is a national organization that defends Americans' civil rights guaranteed in the U.S. Constitution. It adamantly opposes regulation of all forms of speech, including pornography and hate speech. The ACLU offers numerous reports, fact sheets, and policy statements on a wide variety of issues, including the right to privacy, church-state separation, and the government's antiterrorism efforts. Publications include the briefing papers "Freedom of Expression," "Hate Speech on Campus," and "Popular Music Under Siege."

American Library Association (ALA)
50 E. Huron St., Chicago, IL 60611
(800) 545-2433 • fax: (312) 440-9374
e-mail: membership@ala.org • website: www.ala.org

The ALA is the nation's primary professional organization for librarians. Through its Office for Intellectual Freedom (OIF), the ALA supports free access to libraries and library materials. The OIF also monitors and opposes efforts to ban books. The ALA's sister organization, the Freedom to Read Foundation, provides legal defense for libraries. Publications include the *Newsletter on Intellectual Freedom*, articles, fact sheets, and policy statements, including "Protecting the Freedom to Read."

Americans for Computer Privacy (ACP)
website: www.computerprivacy.org

ACP is a broad-based coalition that brings together more than 100 companies and 40 associations representing financial services, manufacturing, telecommunications, high-tech and transportation, as well as law enforcement, civil-liberty, pro-family, and tax-payer groups. ACP supports policies that advance the rights of American citizens to encode information without fear of government intrusion and opposes government efforts to increase widespread monitoring or surveillance. The organization publishes news alerts and issue overviews on its website.

Americans United for Separation of Church and State
518 C St. NE, Washington, DC 20002
(202) 466-3234
website: www.au.org

Americans United for Separation of Church and State is a nonprofit organization that works to defend religious freedom by advocating church-state separation and opposing measures such as mandatory prayer in public schools, tax dollars for parochial schools, and meddling in partisan politics by religious groups. The organization litigates in court cases involving church-state separation. It publishes *Church & State* magazine.

Canadian Association for Free Expression (CAFE)

PO Box 332, Station B, Etobicoke, Ontario M9W 5L3 Canada
(905) 897-7221 • fax: (905) 277-3914
e-mail: cafe@canadafirst.net • website: www.canadianfreespeech.com

CAFE, one of Canada's leading civil liberties groups, works to strengthen the freedom of speech and freedom of expression provisions in the Canadian Charter of Rights and Freedoms. It lobbies politicians and researches threats to freedom of speech. Publications include specialized reports, leaflets, and *The Free Speech Monitor*, which is published ten times per year.

Center for Democracy and Technology (CDT)

1634 Eye St. NW, Suite 1100, Washington, DC 20006
(202) 637-9800
website: www.cdt.org

CDT's mission is to develop public policy solutions that advance constitutional civil liberties and democratic values in the new computer and communications media. Pursuing its mission through policy research, public education, and coalition building, the center works to increase citizens' privacy and the public's control over the use of personal information held by government and other institutions. Its publications include the reports *Broadband Access: Maximizing the Democratic Potential of the Internet* and *Bridging the Digital Divide: Central & Eastern Europe*, as well as issue briefs and policy papers.

Concerned Women for America (CWA)

1015 Fifteenth St. NW, Suite 1100, Washington, DC 20005
(202) 488-7000 • fax: (202) 488-0806
e-mail: mail@cwfa.org • website: www.cwfa.org

CWA is a membership organization that promotes conservative values and is concerned with creating an environment that is conducive to building strong families and raising healthy children. CWA publishes the monthly *Family Voice*, which argues against all forms of pornography.

Electronic Frontier Foundation (EFF)

454 Shotwell St., San Francisco, CA 94110-1914
(415) 436-9333
website: www.eff.org

EFF is an organization of students and other individuals that aims to promote a better understanding of telecommunications issues. It fosters awareness of civil liberties issues arising from advancements in computer-based communications media and supports litigation to preserve, protect, and extend First Amendment rights in computing and Internet technologies. EFF publishes a comprehensive archive of digital civil liberties information on its website.

Electronic Privacy Information Center (EPIC)

1718 Connecticut Ave. NW, Suite 200, Washington, DC 20009
(202) 483-1140
website: www.epic.org

EPIC is a public interest research center that works to focus public attention on emerging civil liberties issues and to protect privacy, the First Amendment, and constitutional values. It supports privacy-protection legislation and provides information on how individuals can protect their online privacy. EPIC publishes the *EPIC Alert* newsletter and the *Privacy Law Sourcebook.*

Enough Is Enough
e-mail: eieca@enough.org
(888) 2Enough
website: www.enough.org

Enough Is Enough is an independent nonprofit organization that works to educate the public and policy makers about the harms of pornography and to protect children from exposure to Internet pornography and online predators. Enough Is Enough publications include a newsletter, the manual *Enough Is Enough "Safe Surfing in the Library,"* and the brochure *Safe Journeys on the Information Superhighway.*

Family Research Council (FRC)
8801 G St. NW, Washington, DC 20001
(202) 393-2100 • fax: (202) 393-2134
e-mail: corrdept@frc.org • website: www.frc.org

The Family Research Council is an organization that believes pornography degrades women and children and seeks to strengthen current obscenity law. It publishes the monthly newsletter *Washington Watch* and the bimonthly journal *Family Policy*, which features a full-length essay in each issue, such as "Keeping Libraries User and Family Friendly: The Challenge of Internet Pornography." FRC also publishes policy papers, including "Indecent Proposal: The NEA Since the Supreme Court Decency Decision" and "Internet Filtering and Blocking Technology."

Freedom Forum
1101 Wilson Blvd., Arlington, VA 22209
(703) 528-0800 • fax: (703) 284-3770
e-mail: news@freedomforum.org • website: www.freedomforum.org

The Freedom Forum is an international organization that works to protect freedom of the press and free speech. It monitors developments in media and First Amendment issues on its website, in its monthly magazine *Forum News*, and in the *Media Studies Journal*, published twice a year.

Morality in Media (MIM)
475 Riverside Dr., Suite 239, New York, NY 10115
(212) 870-3222 • fax: (212) 870-2765
e-mail: mim@moralityinmedia.org • website: www.moralityinmedia.org

Morality in Media is an interfaith organization that fights obscenity and opposes indecency in the mainstream media. It believes pornography harms society and maintains the National Obscenity Law Center, a clearinghouse of legal materials on obscenity law. Publications include the bimonthlies *Morality in Media* and *Obscenity Law Bulletin* and reports, including "Pornography's Effects on Adults and Children."

National Coalition Against Censorship (NCAC)
275 Seventh Ave., New York, NY 10001
(212) 807-6222 • fax: (212) 807-6245
e-mail: ncac@ncac.org • website: www.ncac.org

The coalition represents more than forty national organizations that work to prevent suppression of free speech and the press. NCAC educates the public about the dangers of censorship and how to oppose it. The coalition publishes *Censorship News* five times a year, articles, various reports, and background papers. Papers include "Censorship's Tools Du Jour: V-Chips, TV Ratings, PICS, and Internet Filters."

National Coalition for the Protection of Children & Families
800 Compton Rd., Suite 9224, Cincinnati, OH 45231-9964
(513) 521-6227 • fax: (513) 521-6337
website: www.nationalcoalition.org

The coalition is an organization of business, religious, and civic leaders who work to eliminate pornography. It encourages citizens to support the enforcement of obscenity laws and to close down neighborhood pornography outlets. Publications include the books *Final Report of the Attorney General's Commission on Pornography, The Mind Polluters,* and *Pornography: A Human Tragedy.*

People for the American Way (PFAW)
2000 M St. NW, Suite 400, Washington, DC 20036
(202) 467-4999 or (800) 326-PFAW • fax: (202) 293-2672
e-mail: pfaw@pfaw.org • website: www.pfaw.org

PFAW works to promote citizen participation in democracy and safeguard the principles of the U.S. Constitution, including the right to free speech. It publishes a variety of fact sheets, articles, and position statements on its website and distributes the e-mail newsletter *Freedom to Learn Online.*

Religious Freedom Coalition
PO Box 77511, Washington, DC 20013
website: www.rfcnet.org

The RFC is a conservative Christian coalition, which promotes religious freedom and family values–oriented legislation. It advocates the involvement of religious individuals and organizations in politics. It publishes a newsletter and posts news and legislative updates on its website.

Bibliography

Books

Lee C. Bollinger and Geoffrey R. Stone, eds.	*Eternally Vigilant: Free Speech in the Modern Era.* Chicago: University of Chicago Press, 2002.
Lee C. Bollinger and Geoffrey R. Stone, eds.	*Must We Defend Nazis?: Hate Speech, Pornography, and the First Amendment.* New York: New York University Press, 1997.
Tammy Bruce	*The New Thought Police: Inside the Left's Assault on Free Speech and Free Minds.* Roseville, CA: Forum, 2001.
Nancy Chang et al.	*Silencing Political Dissent: How Post–September 11 Anti-Terrorism Measures Threaten Our Civil Liberties.* New York: Seven Stories Press, 2002.
Thomas J. Curry	*Farewell to Christendom: The Future of Church and State in America.* New York: Oxford University Press, 2001.
James X. Dempsey and David Cole	*Terrorism and the Constitution: Sacrificing Civil Liberties in the Name of National Security.* Washington, DC: First Amendment Foundation, 2002.
Alan M. Dershowitz	*Shouting Fire: Civil Liberties in a Turbulent Age.* Boston: Little, Brown, 2002.
Garrett Epps	*To an Unknown God: Religious Freedom on Trial.* New York: St. Martin's Press, 2001.
Amitai Etzioni	*The Limits of Privacy.* New York: Basic Books, 1999.
Stephen M. Feldman	*Please Don't Wish Me a Merry Christmas: A Critical History of the Separation Between Church and State.* New York: New York University Press, 1997.
Stanley Fish	*There's No Such Things as Free Speech: And It's a Good Thing, Too.* New York: Oxford University Press, 1994.
James W. Fraser	*Between Church and State: Religion and Public Education in a Multicultural America.* New York: St. Martin's Press, 1999.
Simson Garfinkel	*Database Nation: The Death of Privacy in the 21st Century.* Cambridge, MA: O'Reilly, 2001.

Bibliography

Mike Godwin	*Cyber Rights: Defending Free Speech in the Digital Age.* New York: Times Books, 1998.
Nat Hentoff	*The Nat Hentoff Reader.* Cambridge, MA: Da Capo Press, 2001.
Nat Hentoff	*Living the Bill of Rights: How to Be an Authentic American.* Berkeley: University of California Press, 1999.
Alan Charles Kors and Harvey A. Silverglate	*The Shadow University: The Betrayal of Liberty on America's Campuses.* New York: HarperPerennial, 1999.
Joseph Loconte	*God, Government, and the Good Samaritan: The Promise and Peril of the President's Faith-Based Initiative.* Washington, DC: Heritage Foundation, 2001.
Ellen Frankel Paul et al., eds.	*The Right to Privacy.* New York: Cambridge University Press, 2000.
William H. Rehnquist	*All the Laws But One: Civil Liberties in Wartime.* New York: Knopf, 1998.
Timothy C. Shiell	*Campus Hate Speech on Trial.* Lawrence: University Press of Kansas, 1998.
Nadine Strossen	*Defending Pornography: Free Speech, Sex, and the Fight for Women's Rights.* New York: New York University Press, 2000.
Reginald Whitaker	*The End of Privacy: How Total Surveillance Is Becoming a Reality.* New York: New Press, 1999.

Periodicals

Jonathan Alter	"Time to Think About Torture," *Newsweek*, November 5, 2001.
Ivan Amato	"Big Brother Logs On," *Technology Review*, September 2001.
Christopher E. Anders	"They Must Remain Separate," *World & I*, July 2001.
William Beaver	"The Dilemma of Internet Pornography," *Business & Society Review*, Fall 2000.
Mark Chaves	"Going on Faith," *Christian Century*, September 12, 2001.
John Derbyshire	"First Amendment First: Why Hollywood Should Be Left Alone," *National Review*, October 9, 2000.
Edd Doerr	"Jefferson's Wall," *Humanist*, January/February 2002.
Edd Doerr	"Religion and Public Education," *Phi Delta Kappa*, November 1998.
Gregg Easterbrook	"The First Amendment Doesn't Come Without Cost," *Wall Street Journal*, November 5, 2001.
George P. Fletcher	"War and the Constitution: Bush's Military Tribunals Haven't Got a Leg to Stand On," *American Prospect*, January 1, 2002.
David Gelernter	"Will We Have Any Privacy Left?" *Time*, February 21, 2000.

David Glenn	"The War on Campus: Will Academic Freedom Survive?" *Nation*, December 3, 2001.
William Norman Grigg	"The Sultans of Smut," *New American*, April 22, 2002.
Bruce Hoffman	"A Nasty Business," *Atlantic Monthly*, January 2002.
Wendy Kaminer	"Virtual Offensiveness," *American Prospect*, November 19, 2001.
Roger Kimball	"The Case for Censorship," *Wall Street Journal*, October 8, 2000.
Irving Kristol	"Liberal Censorship and the Common Culture," *Society*, September 1999.
Laura Leets	"Should All Speech Be Free?" *Quill*, May 2001.
John Leo	"Don't Tread on Free Speakers," *Newsweek*, November 5, 2001.
Toby Lester	"The Reinvention of Privacy," *Atlantic Monthly*, March 2001.
Loren Lomasky	"Talking the Talk: Have Universities Lost Sight of Why They Exist?" *Reason*, May 2001.
Kenan Malik	"Protect the Freedom to Shock," *New Statesman*, August 13, 2001.
Newsweek	"What Price Security?" October 1, 2001.
Jay Nordlinger	"Getting Aroused: What It Takes to Combat Porn," *National Review*, November 19, 2001.
Geoffrey Nunberg	"The Internet Filter Farce," *American Prospect*, January 1, 2001.
Richard A. Posner	"Security Versus Civil Liberties," *Atlantic Monthly*, December 2001.
Anthony D. Romero	"In Defense of Liberty: Accountability and Responsiveness to Civil Liberties," *Vital Speeches of the Day*, January 1, 2002.
Abraham D. Sofaer and Paul R. Williams	"Doing Justice During Wartime: Why Military Tribunals Make Sense," *Policy Review*, February 2002.
Ray C. Spenser	"Can We Curb the Privacy Invaders?" *USA Today*, March 2002.
Stuart Taylor Jr.	"Wiretaps Are an Overblown Threat to Privacy," *National Journal*, October 6, 2001.
Cathy Young	"God Talk," *Reason*, January 2001.
Wendy Murray Zoba	"Church, State, and Columbine," *Christianity Today*, April 2, 2001.

Index